W9-BVY-558

Dawn Without Darkness

REV. ANTHONY T. PADOVANO

Published by Pastoral Educational Services
(Special Projects Division)

Paulist Press
400 Sette Drive, Paramus, New Jersey 07652

President: Rev. Kevin A. Lynch, C.S.P.
Vice President and Project Director:
Rev. Thomas E. Comber, C.S.P.

Editor and Photographic Selection: Joseph W. Nash
Design: Ron Cutro Associates, Tenafly, N. J.

Picture Credits:
Tony Roberts—Pages: 6, 12, 14, 20, 22, 24, 28, 32, 36, 37
42, 48, 50, 64, 66, 73, 74, 80, 89, cover, end sheets.
Ed Lettau—Pages: 8, 10, 17, 21, 38/39, 52/53, 57, 62, 77, 88
George Hoffmann—Pages: 9, 27, 29, 46/47, 72, 79, 86/87,
90, 91
Bernie Greene—Pages: 55, 68/69, 76, 81, 82
Charles O'Connor—Page 84
Gordon Steen—Page 36
Laurence Linton—Page 63
Thomas J. Connellan—Pages: 18, 19
(Black Star):
Ernest Baxter—Pages: 35, 60/61
John Launois—Pages: 26, 45
Joseph Covello—Page 56
Mike Mauney—Page 58
George Ballis—Page 31
(Sierra Club):
Nancy and Retta Johnston—Page 40
Terry and Renny Russell—Page 71

Photograph of clown on pages 68/69 reproduced through permission of Ringling Bros.-Barnum & Bailey Combined Shows, Inc.

Library of Congress
Catalog Card Number: 77-140085

Color Separations by:
Color Control Corporation, Little Ferry, N. J.

Printed and bound in the
United States of America by
American Book-Stratford Press, New York, N.Y.
G.T.O. Litho Inc., Little Ferry, N. J.

NIHIL OBSTAT:
Rev. Msgr. William F. Hogan, S.T.D.
Censor Librorum

IMPRIMATUR:
+ Thomas A. Boland, S.T.D.
Archbishop of Newark, N. J.
Oct. 1, 1970

The Nihil Obstat and Imprimatur are official declarations that a book or pamphlet is free of doctrinal or moral error. No implication is contained therein that those who have granted the Nihil Obstat and Imprimatur agree with the contents, opinions or statements expressed.

Contents

Preface

Dawn is the most significant moment of the day. It suggests freshness and newness; it engenders ideas of hope and promise. Dawn is a time when night and day meet. Sun, moon, and stars collaborate to give a soft and fragrant light to the world. Dawn is for harmony. It is an hour when many things converge and when everything is just about to begin.

Christmas was given as the night verged toward dawn. Easter is also a dawn experience. This is a book about Christ and Easter, about peace and light, about dawn and about us. It is a book which seeks to tell us something about what happens to us as we go from dawn to dawn, from birth to beyond death, from Christmas to Easter. It is also a book about Jesus. Jesus is one of us. He was made by God to be divine for us.

Jesus was given at Christmas, with dawn approaching, as God's offer of a Son to the human family. Jesus was given as God identified with us in the ordinary experience everyone of us has known: the experience of being born, of a woman, in pain and joy. Jesus was also given to us at Easter, as dawn was born, after he had been given for us on a previous Friday. Jesus was given as God identified with us through an extraordinary experience no one of us has known: the experience of being buried in pain and coming to life in joy.

This is a book of expectations and memories, a book which recognizes darkness but believes in light. It is a book which awaits a dawn without darkness, a dawn when all things shall converge and when everything will be just about to begin forever.

1

The Desert Sands: Waiting

Nothing worthwhile in life is sudden. We wait for birth. We wait for love. We wait for life to reveal its meaning, year by year, experience by experience. Waiting is the law of life, the measure of love.

To wait for another person is to be willing to be alone for him. To wait for someone is to say that the present does not begin until he arrives. To wait together with another is to form a community of hope with him and to affirm the need for another person or a further value essential to the togetherness of those who are vigilant for him.

An understanding of Jesus begins with a theology of patient expectation. Jesus must be awaited. He is not sudden. He comes to patient hearts, to those willing to be alone as they wait, to persons who count the present from his arrival. Jesus is the other awaited by those who form a community of hope and become watchful for the signs of his approach. The advent of Jesus is not limited to Christians. Jesus also gives himself, anonymously, to those who are contemplative about life in devotion to others, to those staggered by the mystery of life and capable of that faith in the future which demands patience. Projects may be rushed; schedules can be accelerated; but life will not be hurried. Jesus comes to hearts patient with hope. Jesus is nearby whenever someone awaits a person or a future worth the waiting.

We must wait to be born. No one is born suddenly. Birth happens to those who have waited in the darkness. Life goes on, as we know, in this darkness. Once darkness is touched by the presence of life, it grows toward the light. And light dawns unfailingly.

Light is God's gift to creation, Christ's grace for every human heart. Light dawns unfailingly. As one is born, he tumbles into the light of this world which, for all its brilliance, is darkness compared to the Light who is God. This Light is immediately given to those who waited for birth but who never came to birth. Light also dawns unfailingly on those who wait in the darkness of death.

No life happens without waiting. This does not mean that one must be quiescent or that life comes to the inactive. We mean that life transcends its present and compels the present to wait for its future. We mean that time-tables serve the momentary and relatively unimportant events of life. Life, however, does not occur on schedule.

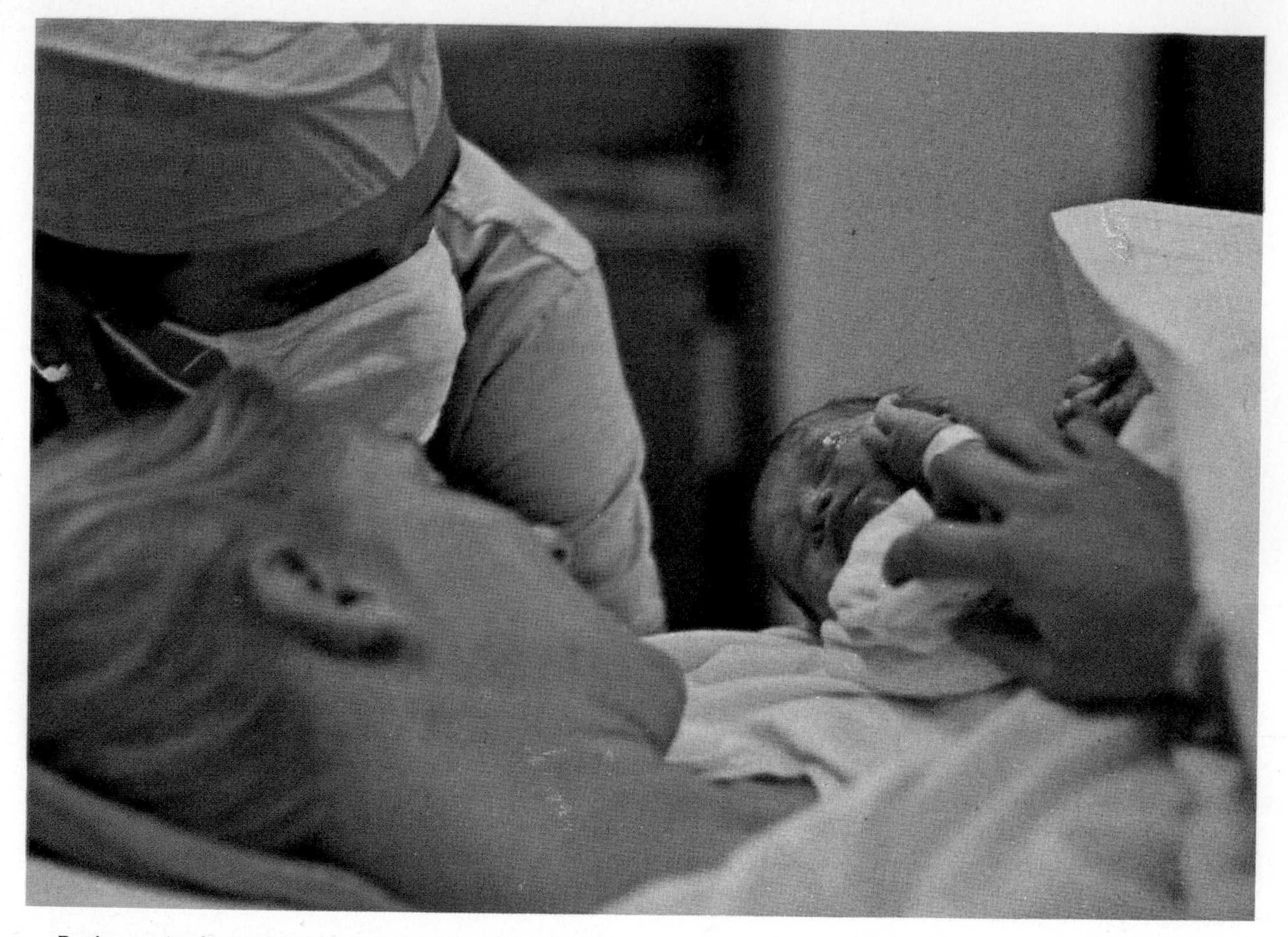

Patience is the restraint essential to the growth of a human person. We wait for life to reveal its meaning not knowing when this meaning shall become clear nor even the specific circumstances through which this meaning will be mediated. We wait in hope, not always aware of which event will justify our hope but unshaken in the conviction that hope will one day be justified.

As life waits to be born, there is silence and darkness, little perceptible activity, a certain alone-ness. One might suppose nothing is happening and yet life, the greatest of all happenings, is happening. It is a time for waiting. Life is waiting to be born. It is enveloped in waiting. As human life awaits birth, the birth of a human person is awaited, in hope, by those who already love this child on his journey from darkness toward light.

Waiting is essential to the life of the spirit as well as to the growth of the flesh. Grace is awaited. The bridegroom opens the door to those prepared to wait; the father who waits finds his prodigal son and knows how to bring him home. We have been told that the watchful are blessed; we have been urged to wait.

Jesus must be awaited. He is awaited by history, by Mary, by all men who have faith in him. Jesus is awaited and he waits. He waits to grow, to be born of Mary, to learn to talk, to meet the Spirit, to fulfill the desert of prayer and fasting. He waits to see who will respond and who will resist, whether some will walk with him no more, who may betray him, and how he shall die.

Those who refuse to wait never become Christians. A Christian must wait with unaccustomed hopes and unconventional love for even more than human love. For, the love which comes to the waiting is not always a human love. A Christian knows Jesus was awaited for a long time; he is prepared to wait another long time for him.

Those who are unable to wait miss those who wish to give themselves to us but who cannot give

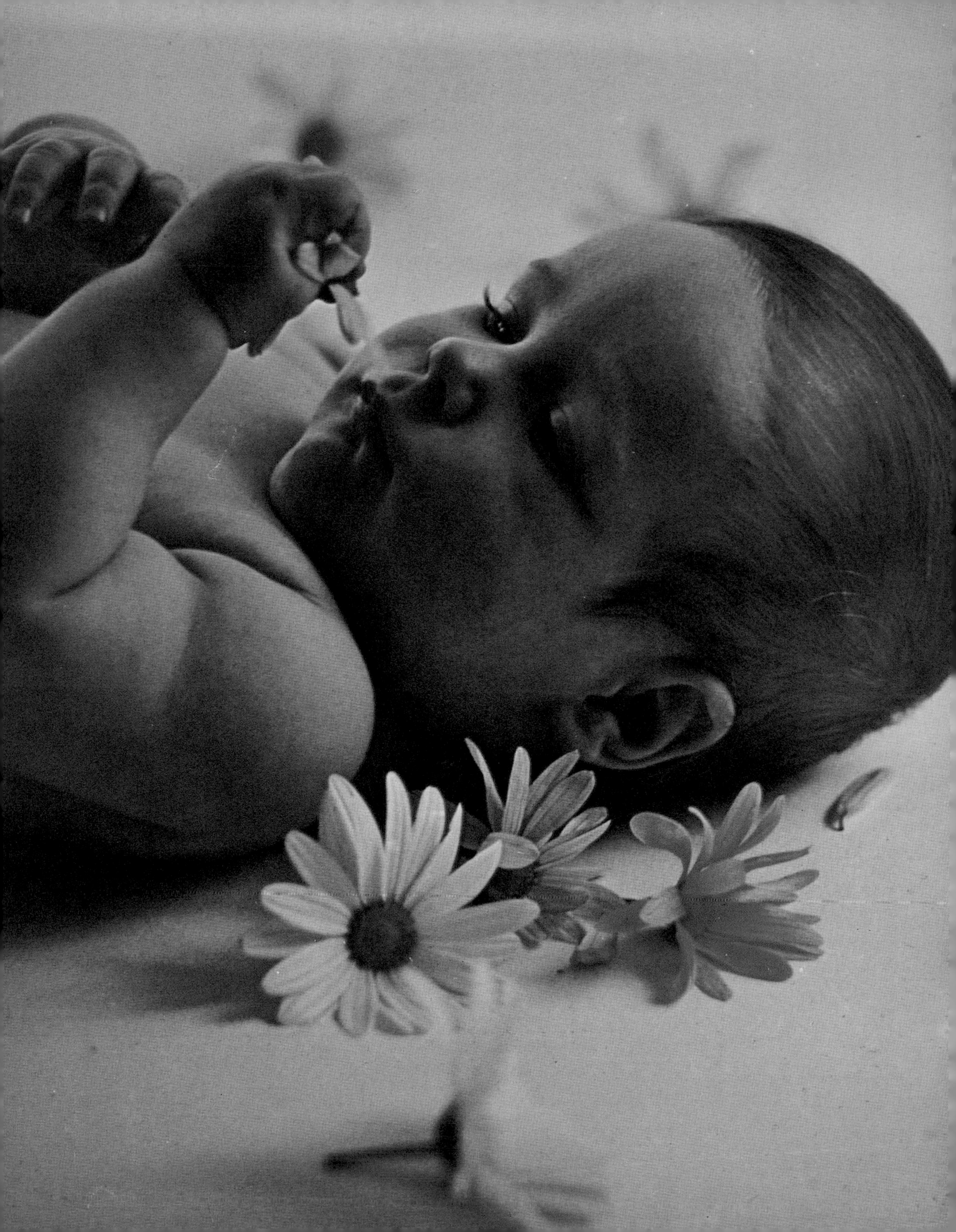

themselves all at once. Those who hurry life refuse others the time they need to become themselves for us and to give all that they become to us. Love may begin in a moment but it happens over many moments. It reveals its presence and its power slowly, at depths neither lover nor beloved suspect in the beginning, through a history of expectation, disappointment, and eventual fulfillment. So vital is this expectation that it enters into the essential structure of human fulfillment.

Expectation allows hope to happen to love and allows love to justify not only its presence but also its promise. Indeed, blessed, happy are they who wait. To wait is to proclaim that life is never all it should be or can be. It is to say that there is more. We declare our attentiveness and offer ourselves in waiting for that which is yet to come. To be rooted only in the present, to believe one can have it all, so to speak, in a hurry, is to confine the mystery of life and the grace of God to a moment or a year or a decade. When men cease waiting, their hopes die, their dreams are dispelled, and their life is over.

Desert sands suggest patient expectation. A desert has not yet fulfilled its promise; it awaits life and symbolizes prolonged waiting for it. Desert sands are a fusion of the possibility of what they could be and of the past buried within them. Desert sands intrigue us and lead us to reminisce about the history they have endured and preserve.

A theology of patient expectation is inseparable from a theology of vivid memory. Christianity is colored by waiting and recall. It is ardent and wistful, encouraged and nostalgic, a mixture of fire and ashes, a vigilant and mindful community.

As Jesus once did, Christianity seeks the desert and the mountains, the lakes and the cities. It prays alone and together. It is in the desert, however, where both Jesus and the Church meet the Spirit for the first time. The Spirit anoints for mission in the desert where men are reminded that life is a patient endeavor, a venture faithful to its memories and committed to watchfulness.

The barrenness of the desert forces us to appreciate life and to cherish it. It makes us rejoice at the sturdy beauty of its tender flowers, to marvel at the endurance of the life which survives its harshness and at the wonder of water which breaks the monotony of sand and sun. One never overlooks life in the desert.

Jesus and Paul, the dominant personalities of the New Testament, prepare for mission in the desert. In the desert, one is struck at the thought that anything is. Away from his fellow-men, one considers how easily life might not have been. Surrounded by the waste of the desert, one wastes nothing. The desert is not a place to live but a retreat where one prepares for future life and becomes thankful for the life he has already lived.

The life of us who wait is a life for us who remember. No man wants to be forgotten; no person is content to be but a moment in the lives of others, a negligible experience, an indifferent influence. As forceful as the urge to live is the desire to be remembered. As insistent as survival is the need to abide with another.

Jesus was no stranger to this profound emotion. He asked us not to forget him. It was his human life he sought to have us remember. Whenever Christians become solemn about their memory of Jesus, they break bread and consecrate wine, repeating the haunting words of the man about to die: "Remember me." Like us, Jesus thought it more imperative to be remembered than to live forever. As he became conscious of his impending death, he gathered around him those least likely to forget. The meaning of his life was bound inextricably to their capacity to remember him.

A man does not achieve fulfillment in his memory of himself but in his being remembered by others. These few who encircled Jesus were those on whose memory so much depended. These who believed must see in his life not the record of a criminal but a yearning to be remembered as one who went about doing good.

Those who recall someone to us do not inspire us unless their memory excites them. A spiritual bond unites those who tell us of someone who meant life itself to them with us who are touched and healed by someone we have never met. Those who love another are anxious to remember; they know that no one truly dies until the memory of

him is erased.

Pentecost was God's coming to strengthen the fidelity of a community to the memory of Jesus. With the Incarnation, the memory of Jesus was begun in flesh and blood with all the attendant mysteries of sonship and virginity, motherhood and celibate fatherhood. The memory of Jesus is now preserved in the Spirit and through a community's faith, with all the attendant mysteries of bread and wine, revelation and tradition.

Jesus was first recognized by those who remembered a prophecy and beheld a star, by those whose memories were transubstantiated into hopes, by those whose gifts symbolized what was and what might yet occur.

When we remember, we leave the present for the past. To say it better, we bring the past into the present and give it life alongside the tangible realities we are compelled to consider. In our memory of another, we choose to relate to him even though, since he is not present, we need not relate to him. Not physical presence but love leads us to live with this remembered person even in his absence. When the love is strong, the memory of this absent person may be more dear and more real than the reality of those who are present. Memory is sometimes the difference between life and death, between hope and despair, between strength for another day and the collapse of all meaning. Our memory of another confers the present upon him, gives him further life in our life, and keeps a moment of the past from drifting away or fading into death. We are fed and nourished by a communion of life in which two lives intersect in memory and merge into a common experience. No lover forgets. No beloved is forgotten. The memory of love is life; the memory of another becomes ourselves.

When the communion of believers remembers Jesus, when the bride is alive with the thought of her Spouse, Christ is present. Jesus is brought into the present with his grace by the force of memory in the power of the Spirit. The Eucharist is a memory made sacrament, a thought rendered in personal presence, a tender moment become flesh and blood. The Eucharist is the Church's act of fidelity to the Jesus who pleaded with us not to forget him.

Every memory of another is a concrete experience. One does not recall generic realities but specific details. One remembers a definite face, certain words, distinctive actions, familiar places. The Church remembers Jesus concretely, with the elements and words of the Lord's Supper. It remembers Jesus at that moment when he asked us most concretely to recall him.

Those who live without memories have missed life. They have nothing worth keeping alive beyond the span of its natural lifetime. They have met no one they wished to abide with forever.

A Church without memories is a Church to whom Christ is not present. Our memory of Jesus makes him present in the Spirit with the intensity of his life, the reality of his presence, the grace of his nearness. Memory is an act of tradition. It is a preservative action by which we refuse to let time pass irrevocably or another to die irretrievably.

There are hours when the Church seems enveloped in darkness or when our own lives have no light. But we are a people who have waited before. We wait knowing that life goes on in the darkness and strains for the light. Life can grow without much motion, without light. After a time, life creates its own light. In its apparent absence, light can enlighten us by the memory of it and by the realization of its inevitable presence.

There are sands in the desert because something once happened there and because all that must come to pass has not yet occurred. The Spirit came to Jesus in the desert. The Spirit shall come to us, if need be, in the wilderness of our hopes and in the bleakness of our present moments. The Spirit is the Father's gift to patient spirits and mindful hearts. The gift of the Spirit is fidelity to the memory of life's mystery and confidence in the mystery of its future.

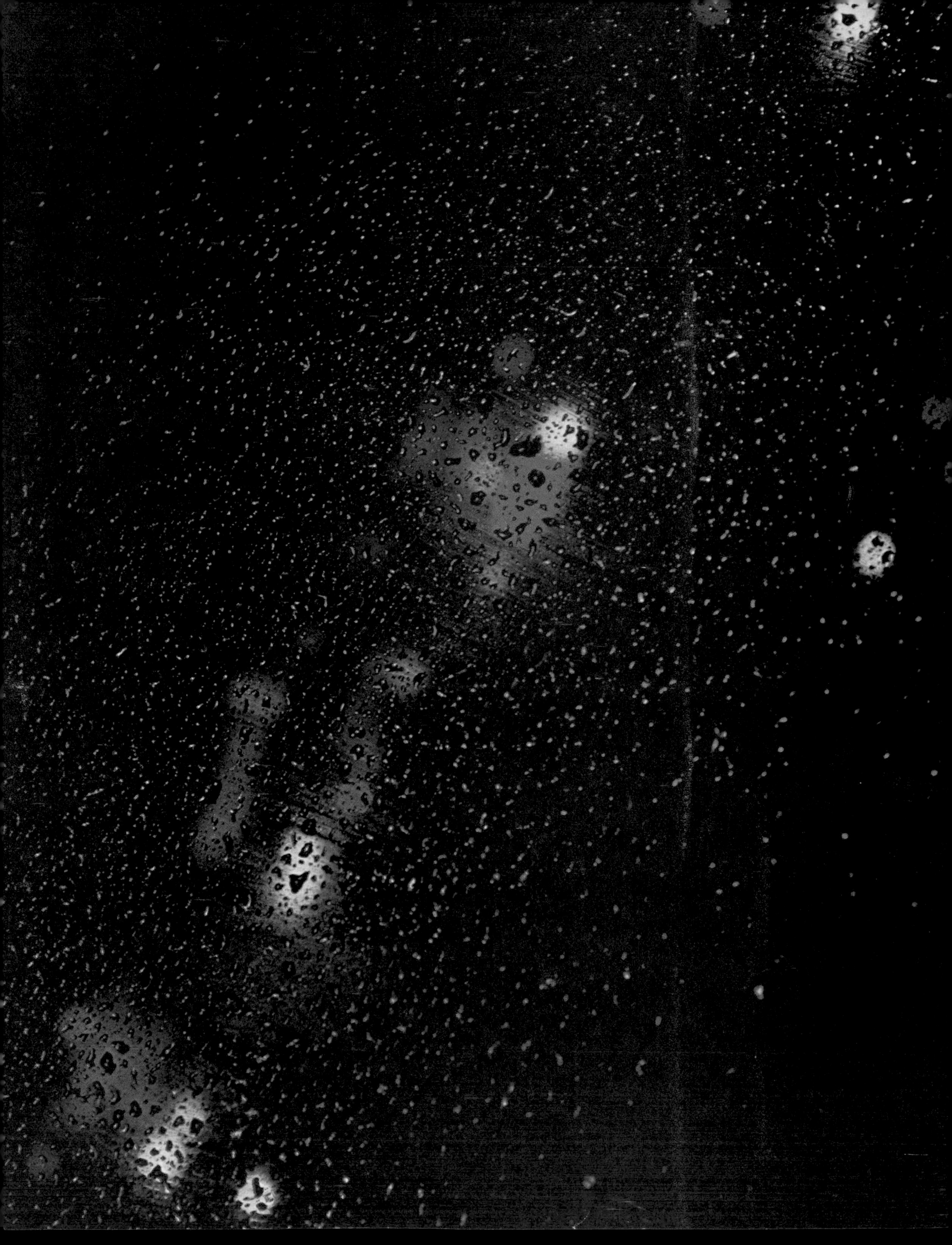

2

A Star-lit Night: Birth

There has not come a day when the sun did not give light. Color has never gone from the earth. History records no day on which a baby has not breathed its first breath. Men have always found the sea when the sands have gone astray. No moment passes without lovers finding one another. Prayer is not forgotten; friendship lasts; men celebrate somewhere everyday. We have learned how to sing; dancing was a human invention. Bread and wine have been made by men who create ritual from the need for nourishment.

One might object that this description of life leaves out the darkness. It neglects the fact that the seas not only enchant but destroy, that love begins but it also ends, that men have rejoiced in the death of their brothers and sisters.

The wonder of life derives from the realization that so few of the really important things go wrong. Most of us suffer distress not in the fact that realities which truly matter go awry but in the frustration of artificial goals, conventional values, arbitrary objectives. This is not to dismiss tragedy but it is to put it into perspective. Few of us need to be reminded that there is terrible pain in life. No man lives long without hurting or bleeding. Almost every man conceals the scars and sometimes the bitterness of a lifetime of injury, rejection, disappointment. This side of life, however, is less than half the story. The tragedies which break our hearts again and again are not more numerous than the healing influences which mend us. More impressive than the broken-ness of our hearts is the fact that we have a heart and that it is tender enough to suffer. Even a scar tells us of more than the wound we have sustained; it tells us that we have prevailed. No agony is sufficient to cancel out the fact that a man was born and that life and thought, emotion and choice, love and reason go on inside him.

Human life is under siege not because so many important things go wrong but because men make lesser values the standard of what human life must become. Human life loses its sacredness not when men abandon an institutional Church but, more decisively, when they build life on values which betray the Father of life and the Lord of the Church. This may occur within or without the periphery of the visible Church.

Of all sins, the most destructive is the sin which makes life the means to a lesser end. Of all blindness, the least curable is the sightless distortion of the grace of life, its resources and capacity. The tragedy of life does not begin with suffering but with the dismissal of the poetry of life as irrelevant. The force of love, the power of tenderness, the strength of gentleness, the glory of color, the warmth of touch are too often taken for granted and spoiled in our anxiety for power or property or wealth.

We give birth to children from the limited substances of our own bodies and wonder whether we have accomplished anything significant in life. A husband and wife remain faithful to each other through years of joy and anguish, tension and harmony, brilliant days and bitter nights. They may then be disheartened in their love because a promotion never came through or a better home was not purchased or because a son failed to gain entrance to the best possible college. Sometimes these minor realities are made the measure of a man's success as a husband or a woman's adequacy as a wife. Every culture knows of the happiness and love a man and woman create for each other. It would require an enormous amount of explanation to men of another culture or age to explain that one's sense of failure derives from the fact that one's home was too small or his office was on the lower floor of an executive building or that one's son settled for the wrong college.

We must not simplify the problem. Other cultures also have their arbitrary standards. Besides, we are not disembodied spirits. We are, therefore, influenced by the values society sets as standards of excellence and achievement. Each man seeks a means by which he may measure his worth. We are pointing out, however, that our culture, every culture, devises criteria for success and happiness which do not correspond with the gift of life. No criterion, except love or life, is adequate to life. The demonic influence in life is evident whenever an age or a culture takes seriously the non-essential elements of life and takes for granted the realities by which life reveals its presence and purpose. This reversal of values is our original and persistent sin.

We have become so beguiled with the compulsion "to do" that many of us consider it a waste of time "to be". So often it is argued that it is unproductive "to be", that one must always make something of himself, which generally means that one must make money. How do we judge a human being as a success or as a person of worth? How many of us have the courage and the candor to put into words what it is which makes us pay more attention to one person rather than another? When we speak our foolishness out loud it appears even more absurd. Why do we "cultivate" some people and disregard others?

Not only personal relationships but life itself is mishandled. Why is it stupid to walk in the rain? Why do we neglect autumn or await the seasons with resignation rather than anticipation? The luxuries we claim we cannot afford are the luxuries of existence, the luxury of sensing our alive-ness and allowing it to express itself. If we would compose the epitaph by which we want to be remembered, many of us would realize that the success we prefer in life is not the success we are seeking.

Contemplation is impossible when life becomes an unimportant value. Devotion dies when love is desired but never given. Poetry perishes in the postponement of dreams until the day when they shall favor us with practical results. The fact that we have the capacity to communicate with another human being on the deepest levels of his life means less to some than the next promotion or a more spacious driveway. The message of the Gospel is this: no achievement is worth as much as the mystery by which one person comes to know and to love another.

We question, do we not, whether a good man living to the potential of his goodness can prevail. We ask about this and Jesus of Nazareth lived here. Has an evil man ever lasted? Has someone who has done less with life than Jesus did influence life more? Why was Jesus successful as a human being?

Jesus did not accept the arbitrary standards of his day. He sought no place of power; he refused kingship; he bought no home; he praised mercy over sacrifice, need over the suffocation of wealth; he preferred the lilies of the field to political favor. Jesus lived life. He was no slave to the

conventional values of either a Judaic or a Roman system.

Jesus lived life. He gave himself to those who needed him rather than to those who had all they needed. He was concerned with a few loaves and fishes, with prophecy and Fatherhood, faith and flowers. He cared for these realities because he sought to reveal life's deepest meaning. We can dismiss his message but we should not do this while we call ourselves Christians unless, of course, we are not troubled by our own hypocrisy.

Christians are inconsistent when they maintain that the life-style of Jesus was suitable for Jesus but not for us. We are short-sighted when we claim we shall accept the doctrine of Jesus but not his behavior. We seldom seek to correct the doctrine of Jesus; we more easily refine and excuse his behavior. Yet Jesus reveals less in his words than in his life-style. And he reveals not only who God is but what a man must become.

We have a tendency to dismiss Jesus as a dreamer or to dismiss him as divine. We write off, at times, the human effort and the human achievement of the life of Jesus by resorting to his Sonship with God. Some of us disregard the human life of Jesus so that we might remain complacent, calling ourselves his disciples, repeating his words, but avoiding his life-style.

The great challenge of our day is not orthodoxy in doctrine but heroism in action. Fidelity to Jesus in both word and deed is, of course, important. No witness reaches our contemporaries more persuasively, however, than the witness of Christians who do what Jesus did.

We become impoverished in our Christian mission because we attend to the parables of Jesus but not to his poverty, to the catechesis of the New Testament but not to its standards of life. Few today leave the Church because they are troubled with an article of the creed. The crippling, sinful, insidious heresy of our day has been the heresy by which we have denied the way Jesus lived as normative for the way we must live. Many have affirmed the divinity of Jesus as an escape. After all, one cannot imitate the divinity of Christ. As long as this divinity is made largely responsible for the human magnitude of Jesus, we manage to hold ourselves excused from living as he lived.

How did Jesus live? He lived by taking as his standard many of the values we affirmed in the opening sentences of this chapter. Yet had there not followed, in the second paragraph, some modification of what was expressed in the first, many Christians would have considered the words to have been the words of an idealist or an "unrealist."

Jesus did not allow himself to be rendered ineffective by pursuing the pretensions of his day. He looked into the human heart and was careful not to neglect the color of the earth and the mystery of the heavens. These formed the values of his life.

We escape the demands of the life of Jesus on us when we relate to him in prayer but not in action. For some, the "spiritual" life has become the most deadly and subtle way of rejecting Jesus. They are blind to the vision of Jesus who are hypnotized by the pagan values of their culture or even by the pagan values of an ecclesiastical society. T. S. Eliot reminds us that those who serve the greater cause may make that cause serve them. To transform the Gospel into a conventional value, to profess the faith as an arbitrary objective, to confuse a confession of Jesus with an artificial goal is to sin against the Spirit.

How many of us Christians have paganized the Church with our ecclesiastical privileges, our jealousy for authority and power, our self-serving servility? How many Christians have de-sacralized the Church by using prayer as an escape, by ex-

ploiting others with our piety, by demanding consistency with the doctrine of Jesus but not with his values? How many have exalted the divinity of Jesus so that his human life might no longer accuse them? How many of us are on this path of perdition? How many of us have compromised the Gospel, not always conscious of what we were doing and yet sufficiently aware of the comfort with which we surrounded ourselves at the expense of other lives and other hopes?

We scarcely know what it means to give our lives for life. We have become Christians, too often, not because we were disciples of Jesus but because we could not bear to become the enemies of Jesus openly. We have remained Christians, at times, because we gained the best of two worlds, forgetting the warning of Jesus that these two worlds could not be reconciled.

We shall become Christians on that day when sunshine means more to us than a further acquisition. We shall become Christians on that day when the children of the world excite us at least as much as its rulers. We shall become Christians on that day when we use our hearts to measure the worth of a human being, on that day when greed or pride do not lead us to friendship but only love.

We shall become Christians when we are joyful because so many people are in love rather than because so many people are affluent. We shall become Christians when we learn to make music and poetry, to make love and peace, to make Jesus human and to make ourselves as human as he was. We shall become Christians when the sight of the sea makes us dance more joyously than the purchase of a new car. We shall become Christians when we allow Jesus to speak to us by his values as well as by his words. We shall become Christians on that morning when we laugh and sing for the right reasons and when we weep not because we have lost something but because we were given so much.

3

Home: Yearning

The difference between a world of fantasy and a kingdom of hope is a dream.

In this chapter, we shall distinguish between wishes, hopes and dreams and show how they enter into the process by which men yearn for home-coming.

One of the first distinctions we must make is that between wishes and hopes. Life is not hopeful because wishes are granted. Hope derives from a reasonable foundation; wishes are flights of fancy, often leading us to want the unattainable. Hope is the fruit of a mature heart; wishes are the uncertain expressions of that in us which has not yet come of age.

In spite of this, it is good that we make wishes. There is no problem in having wishes; there is, in building a life upon them. Although life is a serious endeavor, not everything in life is serious. Wishes remind us that life can be earnest without becoming grim, that our emotions may often desire things our reason knows we shall never have. Wishes make us playful with life and suggest that reason need not mean everything. Men wish because they choose to live with more than sturdy certitudes, reasonable desires, responsible hopes. Wishes teach us that we could have been something or someone other than who we are. We become who we are not because we exhaust our potential in one direction but because we take one path and not another. Hopes build upon who we actually are and, granting this, on what we are able to become. Wishes make us sensitive to the fact that we might have become something totally different from what is now possible. Wishes are the result of the unused energy in us which would have been expended had our life gone another way.

God is not someone who grants our wishes; he is someone who fulfills our hopes. God does not make wishes come true; he makes reality work. He sustains us not in our whimsical desires but in our mature choices. As we shall see later, the difference between a man of faith and the man of no faith is the difference between a man who hopes for home and the man who wishes for home.

Jesus wished he might not have to die; he had no real hope that the cross could have been avoided. He wished that Jerusalem had not murdered the prophets and that it had listened to the

prophet who now wept for Jerusalem's inability to fulfill its promise, to recognize its own children, to make a home for its sons. What Jerusalem might have been! Jerusalem was a symbol of the world. What the world might have been! There was a certain consolation in the conjecture and in the wish. But Jerusalem must be Jerusalem. It might have heard the prophets but there seemed little hope that it would heed this prophet. And so even without hope one might weep at the wish of what might have been. In doing this, Jesus loved Jerusalem with more than hope and went to his death in the hope that not all his wishes for Jerusalem would be incapable of hope, that somehow Jerusalem would hear his death and heed his pain and from his very flesh and blood listen to the Word he sought to speak.

Wishes, as we have said, are beneficial as long as we do not build a life or build hope upon them. Some lose hope because their wishes are not granted. This is ironically tragic because hope gives us strength to continue during those moments when our dreams are dispelled and our every wish appears impossible. There are times when we run out of wishes; hope, however, is inexhaustible. Jesus taught us this. Death might mean the end of all our wishes; it need not be the finish of all our hopes. The wish of Jesus that he might not die died with him. The hope that death would serve, that it would redeem, that it would be received, continued. Jesus died without wishes but in the hope that his Father would not be absent in death. Jesus took hope into death, which was once thought to be a force stronger than hope. This hope of Jesus, which passed through death, was fashioned from the demise of all the human hopes of Jesus. It was a hope strangely brought to life as Jesus shed his blood in sacrifice and gave his life in love.

The cross was not a place for dreams; every wish for rescue and further life was rendered vain by the forsake-ness of Calvary; but hope was born from the cross. This hope had no need of wishes; it was a hope stronger than death, a hope substantial with Fatherhood and absolutely unshakeable in its conviction that death was but another way to come home. Christ is the Father's sign to us of how fully Jesus came home, of how totally he fulfilled his destiny, of how deeply he was reconciled to himself and to us. Christ is the Easter greeting with whom the Father renders Judgment, gives mercy, and welcomes us home to Jerusalem. The Jerusalem over which Jesus wept and wished is the Jerusalem which has justified the hopes of Christ.

We have yet a word to speak concerning dreams. Hopes derive from a reasonable foundation and give life. Wishes are flights of fancy, momentary and inconsistent desires; they are conjectures of what might have been, fashioned sometimes at the precise moment when we know there is no hope of their fulfillment. Dreams refer to the visions of life with which we live, visions composed of hopes and wishes, visions constant and consistent enough for us to work for their realization and build a kingdom upon them. By dreams, we mean a vision of life worth the effort, never impossible of achievement nor certain of accomplishment. Wishes need never be realized; hopes are always fulfilled; dreams or visions are worthy of faith, always capable of sustaining reality, but not always becoming reality. Dreams or visions are an indication of how life will go and can go. Jesus wished he might not die; he hoped his death would have meaning; he may easily have dreamed that no one of his friends would forsake him. It was inevitable that Jesus would encounter the hatred of his enemies; it was certain to Jesus that his death would not be in vain; there was no need, however, for Jesus to be deserted by his own.

The fidelity of the disciples would not have been impossible. The most painful of all betrayals is the betrayal which serves no purpose and is essential to no plan. Jesus would have died and redeemed, hoped and reigned even in the fidelity of his friends. It was not only the body but the dreams of Jesus which were shattered on the cross.

We might console ourselves with the thought that, after all, our wishes had little chance of coming true. With dreams, it is different. They might so easily have come true; there is seldom a good reason why they do not come true. Men

are led to the brink of despair by the failure of their dreams. It is then that hope must assure us that, although things might easily have gone one way and did not, they shall yet accomplish a purpose and bring us home. We may be certain that this hope will come to pass and yet so uncertain as to how this shall be accomplished that we are not able to fashion a dream from it. Hope survives even the vanishing of our dreams and remains as the germ of those further dreams born from our common future.

Never to dream, not to have visions is not to live. To dream of what shall never come to pass is an indication that we have more life in us than one lifetime can exhaust, enough hope in us for infinite dreaming. Jesus was not only someone who did good deeds but someone who dreamed of things which never came to pass.

A prophet is a man with a dream. He must envision those possibilities life can accomplish even if it never accomplishes them. A man is an effective prophet if he keeps men dreaming even after the disillusionment of their dreams and the frustration of their wishes. A prophet holds out to men better alternatives, real alternatives, hopeful alternatives, alternatives so complete in their number that one can expend a lifetime in their pursuit and in the hope of their accomplishment. Even when a dream does not come true, a man is better for having dreamed it. A prophet gives men dreams which are not wild fantasy but possibilities even though they may never become realities. A prophet has achieved his destiny when he engenders hope and when he makes men dream of what they may yet become even though they may never become what they could have been.

Prophecy is the means by which our fellowmen stir in our hearts the vague dreams or ardent longings in which we recognize ourselves. In this sense, Jesus was a prophet. He led us to dream of a world in which mercy would be given not only

by God but also by every man. He told us of the peace which was God but also of his dream of a world of peace-makers. Jesus revealed to us that forgiveness even at the hands of one's executioners heals more effectively than hatred. This revelation is the implicit beginning of a dream in which every injury is forgiven. God will always make sense out of man; prophets remind us of further possibilities within us as we await the hope which God never denies. Prophets help us build dreams around our hopes.

To dream of what shall never come to pass is to dream in the manner of Jesus. To dream only of what shall come to pass is to become a wise planner, someone who projects accurately. To dream also of those things which may not likely occur but of which men are capable is to be a prophet, a disciple of Jesus.

For all these reasons, we maintain that the difference between a world of fantasy and a kingdom of hope is a dream.

We must yet discuss home-coming. All the yearning of man points home. Wishes, hopes, and dreams come home with man. But what does it mean to come home?

Home is not a place; it is an attitude. It is an attitude which depends upon how much we are able to feel at home with ourselves as well as with others. Home is something which happens to a person; homecoming has less to do with geography than it has to do with a sense of personal integrity or inner wholeness. The most important of all endeavors in life is to come home. The most terrifying of fears is loneliness. It means that one has become a stranger to himself and, consequently, to others. To be lonely is to feel fear, to be forever unsettled, never at rest, in need of more reassurance than life can give. Someone truly loves us when he brings us home, when he makes us comfortable with ourselves, when he takes from us the strangeness we feel at being who we are. We are loved when we are no longer frightened with ourselves.

The human heart was made to be at home with itself. It is this aspiration which is at the heart of all yearning. We wish for home as our first wish, hope for home until our last hope, dream of home

with every dream we form. We cannot bear to be strangers. We are able to be a pilgrim people for a time but not forever. Should this occur, our wishes would cease, our hopes would die, our dreaming would stop. Yearning for anything would become a mockery since that for which we yearn first and most would be denied us. We would despair with a despair from which there would be no recovery.

The most redemptive of all experiences is that by which the human heart is reconciled with itself. Evil comes from fear and fear comes from an inability to live with oneself, to make a truce with one's own life, to settle the conflict which goes on inside the person who cannot find a home and who never comes home.

Our sins begin when we are unable to feel at home anywhere. We rage at the world because we are angered at ourselves. We exploit others because we do not know how to recognize the limitations of our own hearts. We abuse the bodies of others with sex or violence because our own body is not sacred for us.

Original sin split man's heart in two, divided man against himself, tore his serenity from him, made him his own worst enemy. Because of original sin, man went into history without a home; he was left lonely, longing for someone to come home to, someone to make him unafraid again. Man, the stranger, begins his yearning with wishes, hopes, and dreams of coming home. Of all yearnings, the most powerful, the most painful, the most beneficent is this yearning to come home.

Jesus promised us a home. A day will come, he believed, when we shall be called by name, when we shall rush from our prodigal ways and sense the strength of a father's arms around us. A day will come when no door will be sealed against us. One day, our apparently unheard knocking shall yield to welcome as all the doors open to us in love and peace.

Jesus gave a promise when he taught us to say "Abba, Father," "Our Father." He left us not homeless but, as he said, to prepare a home for us. Even the Judgment is described in terms of home-coming, warmth, greeting for those who shall no longer wander:

> Come, you, there, you, friend, blessed, happy, you who will never again have to leave home. Come, never again shall you know a wrong turn, a strange night, an unfamiliar path, a loss of direction, an alien face. Come, no more shall you need a father, search for a family, long for a brother, miss a sister's love. Come, this is home. After so many fears to the contrary, you are saved, you are healed, you belong. Come, you are safe. We know you, you are ours, we are yours. Come home. Come, you are needed. Come home.

The difference between a man of faith and a man who has no faith depends upon how much of a home one hopes to discover. The distinction between grace and its absence must be drawn in terms of whether we can believe we shall ever come home.

Jesus was masterful in his ability to describe heaven and God as a response to the wants and sometimes lost dreams of his contemporaries. The kingdom is like a net thrown into the sea which comes back full. It is like a lost sheep one has just found, a handful of seed which takes strong root. It is like a son one never thought he would meet again and whom, all of a sudden, one can hardly contain.

The difficulty some of us encounter in feeling at home with ourselves comes from our wishing life to be what it was never meant to be. We have already indicated some of the attitudes which form a path home. Life is an experience of patient expectation and vivid memory. It sets its own standards for home-coming, standards which deny home to those who subjugate life to lesser values than life itself. Possessions, social conventions, earning power are the playthings of fools when they are used to take the measure of the human heart in love or the magnitude of human life in grace.

One never comes home until he prefers a gentle heart to mastery of other lives. One comes home when he learns how to bring a gift and to receive one. One is home when he gives mercy, makes peace, hurts for justice. One is homeward-bound when he is more tormented by the death of innocence than by the frustration of his ambitions. One makes a home everytime he allows a man to feel at home with himself. One is on the right road, not far away, close enough to run the last mile, when he realizes that the greatest of all gifts to give another is home and that the most surprising of all gifts to receive is home-coming.

4

The Dusty Roads of Nazareth: A Child's Vision

Unless he is spoiled, man is a natural poet. Life sings in him, rejoices and glories in him. Man is poet enough to count the stars although knowing their number can do him no good. He is forever struggling up a mountain and plunging into the sea so that he might behold the wonder and the greatness of things.

If man is left to his own resources, he is naturally religious. Something in him makes devotion necessary. This devotion may not always deal with God explicitly or with formal faith. Man, however, needs devotion to someone or something for his own completion.

We are, furthermore, instinctively contemplative. The grace or power of life, its nostalgia or agony compel us to seek silence and to reflect. The human heart responds to beauty with the amazement of its own sensitivity and with the marvel of its own beauty. Life overwhelms us as it surrounds us with safety and suffering. It forces us to sense its sheer massiveness. Life leaves us inadequate before the immeasurable adequacy and transcendental energy which it radiates. At such moments, we become contemplative. We become children again in our hearts; the visions of our early years return; once again, we are stunned by beauty, astounded by the presence of life. Man is instinctively contemplative. At a moment's notice, he is wistful; in the consciousness of anguish, he withdraws fearfully into himself and questions the purpose of his existence.

We have said that man is naturally religious. This spontaneous religious quality of the human heart is never dormant. It may not express itself in traditional religious categories but it reveals its presence in the poetry, the devotion, and the contemplation without which man cannot live a human existence.

There are two ways of going about the religious enterprise. One of these is to create religious experience in the hope of God's grace and by means of the Church's tradition, doctrine and worship. In this case, man is given an environment which makes him conscious of his religious nature and enables him, in grace, to respond in a more or less ordered fashion. Such a man either becomes religious as he confronts this milieu so that the visible Church, as it were, precedes him or he senses the force of God within himself and relates this to the tradition, doctrine, and worship of the visible Church which now, as it were, succeeds him. In either sequence, religious experience is given ecclesial expression and made a sign of faith for the sake of our fellow-men.

There is another way of experiencing faith or sensing grace and religious reality. In this case, the elements which evoke an unstructured religious response are considered. The norm is not the specific life of a distinctive Church but the person who is struggling with faith, yearning for it but who, in all likelihood, will not bring this faith to explicit ecclesial expression.

The Church is most effective when it maintains a dialogue not only with those who enter into its fellowship but also with those who are passionate about faith but tentative about its ecclesiality. Moreover, this dialogue is beneficial for the human family which has always been and will always be concerned with belief. History requires a community of those who are endowed with a tradition and a history of faith and who seek in doctrine to keep misconceptions at a minimum and in worship to form a community from believers.

Some "religious" experience is neither religious nor Christian. A responsible judgment is in order concerning the possibility of "faith" to mediate life and express itself in love. Conversely, the Church ought not enter the dialogue as an exclusively normative agent. It seeks to learn as well as to teach, to be attentive to Christ in this unfamiliar experience as well as to make a believer attentive to Christ from its own experience. The servant Church is obliged to offer the wisdom of its tradition, the insights of its doctrine, the enlightenment of its worship to this person who has felt faith's force but who can give it neither a proper name nor adequate expression.

This latter approach to religious experience is more congenial to our own age. It offers the individual person a larger context in which to evaluate his faith. It offers the Church the enrichment of newness and an opportunity to affirm fidelity to Christ without rigidity. It permits the Church to live without that pretension which tempts the Church to suppose it is the total measure of Christ and that it has already discovered Christ in every way in which Christ shall reveal himself in history.

We have discussed as a more serious challenge for the Church not the precision of its orthodox expression but heroism in action. To simplify, truth is less the issue than love. Of course, the best of all possible worlds is the one which fuses both truth and love into a perfect harmony. To be consistent with the theme of this chapter, we observe that those who leave the Church are most often those who discover the Church has no place for them rather than that the Church teaches falsely. The truth of the Church does not fail because its creeds are ill-formed, or because Scripture is imperfect but because so few act on them. Some of our faithful contemporaries believe that the Church has forgotten to listen, that it learns only too late or only after people have expended enormous amounts of energy.

To be at home in the Church means that one should feel somewhat the same way as he does when he feels at home with his family. One does not remain with his family if he is not heard or listened to or if he gains attention only when he makes an enormous effort or if he is loved merely when he happens to agree with his family. Such a person sooner or later leaves his family either actually walking away or remaining physically but having no heart for this "home" in which he lives. Nor is one part of a family, truly at home, if his self-expression is allowed only if it agrees with that which the family has already experienced and, therefore, can recognize as its own. There is a way, it seems, for a family to remain faithful to its identity and history, to its purpose and significant life-style and yet find room for every legitimate innovation.

We might ask ourselves where we can find the religious energy which no doubt is active in our day as it has been in all the ages of history. What are the raw materials from which men might form an act of faith which is both contemporary and faithful to Christ in its expression? What are the forces which are at work in the human heart to provide sufficient matter for faith, forces which are active because the Spirit renews our restlessness for God? If man is to be responsive to God in this century, how shall he respond? How is

dimensions of man make themselves felt, the more he wishes to talk, to share, to come upon a community which will take seriously what he has come to know as he learns to take a community seriously in what it already knows and seeks to learn.

Unless he is spoiled, man is a natural poet. A child becomes a poet without having been taught. A child is playful with life and reverent in its presence. The most effective persons we meet in life are those who never get over their childhood. Life never really begins for the human heart until it beholds beauty and deems it worth remembering.

A child or a poet is sensitive to experience as a crucial factor in relating to life. Experience is the most immediate consciousness of reality which we have. It tells us what happens to us when we touch reality. Experience is the record and impression of the world on a human being; it is that

modern man an object and a means of God's grace in a way which makes him sacramental in his being and contemporaneous in his existence?

The answer to some of these questions can be discovered in the poetic nature, devotion-potential, and contemplative character of man. Man today is seldom formally religious in his initial response to faith; he is first radically religious and, later, may seek to express this in a formal manner. He encounters the Church in dialogue, not expecting the Church to verify or negate too quickly what he has come to realize. He hopes that the Church will find room for him as he opens himself, tentatively, to the mystery of the Church.

The forces of poetry, devotion, and contemplation aspire to an act of faith which affirms the religious meaning they contain and leaves the person free to develop simultaneously self-expression and integration into the tradition, doctrine, and worship of a believing community. The stronger the poetic, devotional, contemplative

which happens to a person as he begins to see and hear, to converse with and wonder about the reality in which we live. Experience happens when the child in us runs free into the world and takes the shock of its pain and its joy. It is an implicit act of reason, a perception not learned but lived, assimilated into one's flesh and blood rather than by his intellect. It can, of course, be misused as can reason or will. Nothing, including the Gospel or even God, is impervious to our misuse. Yet, for all this, experience, immediacy with life is what we need desperately today not only to be secular in a human way but also to be religious in a Christian manner.

There is no such thing as a poet who is not open to the transcendent. Every poet has heard the song of mystery which life is and sings his response, sometimes in measured words, sometimes in broken syllables, sometimes, like a dancer, with the rhythm of his own body, sometimes with the tears in his eyes, the laughter of his heart, the searching touch of someone who loves and is loved. No poet is bound to one age of history, confined to a country, entangled in only one world, be it secular or sacred. Every poet strains for the mystery beyond all the mystery of life, the song which makes us all sing, the light which, without physical presence, illumines life itself. If we have lost touch with the transcendent and gratuitous in life, lost contact with God and the gift of his nearness, if we have wandered so far from life that we can no longer believe it has a Creator or that the Creator has grace to give, this has happened because we have ceased being poets. Man is a natural poet; every poet is instinctively religious.

No man is a Christian unless he preserves a sense of wonder. Americans once began with this sense of wonder but as our history developed we tended to lose it. The vestiges of its presence can

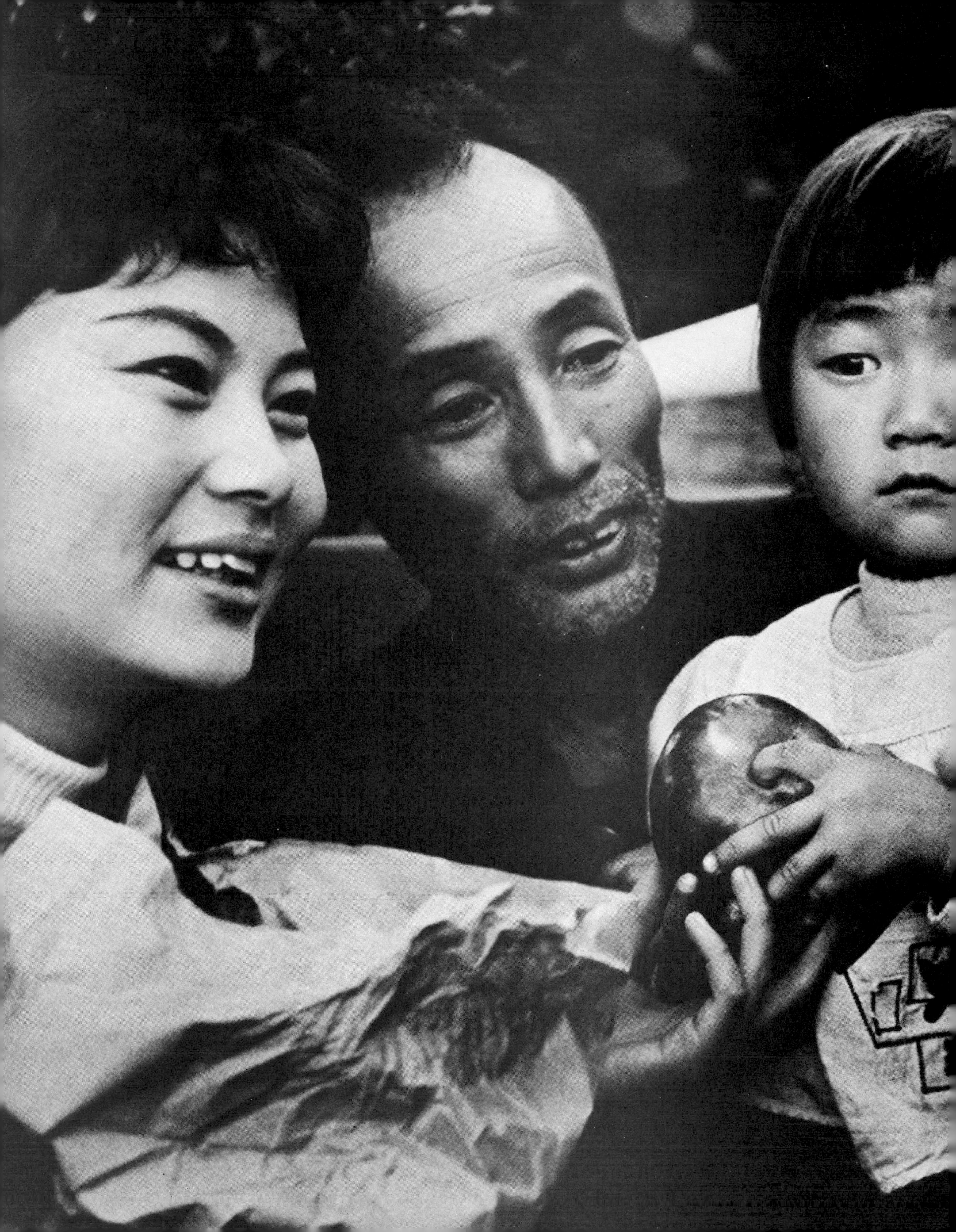

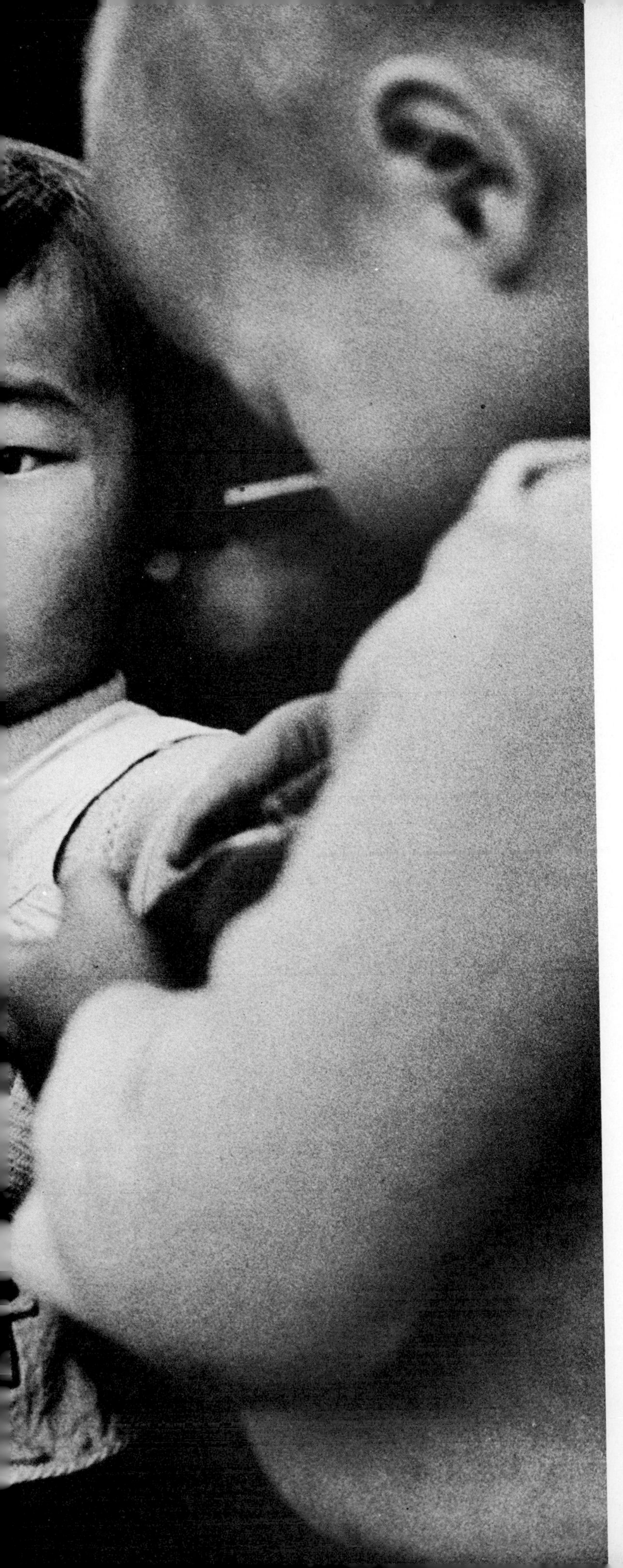

still be felt. Once we believed in freedom, in the paradise we had inherited, in the God who marked our violence with regret but who gave us a new land, a continent, in which to wonder. Americans sought the expansion of their experience with the pragmatic method and with technological ingenuity. Now, however, we need someone to save us from the religious pretentiousness of the things we have made, a savior to rescue us from the lesser saviors we manufacture. We must become poets again, poets who treasure their technology but poets who give technology second place. We must become poets who see what technology once sought to enhance but eventually supplanted. Technology has taken us from the naturalness of life.

We have become like the child who has too many gifts and who no longer plays with any of them. We must put aside our toys and touch life again. We must become poets or else we shall die. We must become poets so that our efficiency will cede again to tenderness and so that we might come to feel life rather than manage it. We must become poets who are no longer strangers to their emotions, no longer afraid of their tears, hesitant with laughter, ill at ease with affection.

In our day, sexual experience has become so important because for many people it is the most meaningful natural reality left in a world of steel and calculation. For many, it is the last touch with nature, the greenness of life in the midst of the asphalt of our existence, the tree which grows in Brooklyn. Some become desperate about sexual expression because they sense that if they lose this, they may lose the experience of what it means to feel like a human being.

We must become poets who establish ties again with life, growing reverent with the forces of life which surround us in the universe. A poet does not need life to go a certain way in order to appreciate it; he needs only its presence.

Aristotle once wrote that the nature of man is not what he is born *as* but what he is born *for*. Man was not born to wonder at technology but to sense life, to become devoted to it, and contemplative about it.

Man's act of faith begins with the poetry of his

heart and it leads him to become devoted to the poetry in the heart of another. Devotion is our way of singing a song another can hear and of hearing the song another sings. Every poet is a man of devotion, one who not only responds to the beauty in the midst of which he lives but one who gives himself with all the beauty he can create into the keeping of another.

Unless he is spoiled, man is naturally devoted. He does not sing alone nor create beauty alone. He writes for the sake of his fellow-men and for the sake of that almost terrible force of the transcendent which he feels within him and which makes him suffer until he makes a song.

The air a poet breathes is the air of devotion. No man makes an act of faith without devotion. And devotion must be given to a person, never to an idea or to a Church as such or to God as a concept or a system. Devotion is for persons. The man who is blind to persons lives without poetry, without devotion, and, always, without faith. God is God because he is three persons, expressing in himself the poetry of love, the fullness of life, and the devotion involved in all personal relationships.

The meaning of life depends, then, not on what one possesses but on what one sees in that which he possesses. A child is someone who seeks to look Into the nature of the things he possesses. A poet is someone who looks inside.

To look deeply inside life, one must be devoted to another person so that he can perceive and possess the heart of another. Until one becomes devoted to a person, he sees only the inside of things. This is why every poet is a lover or else his poetry dies. And every man of faith is a man of devotion or else his faith dwindles into doubt and denial.

The greatness of Jesus depended upon what he saw in the same human experiences we undergo. He became contemplative because he saw the Father in the wheat fields and in the stars, in the lilies and in the sheep, in the lake with its fish, in the harvest with its fruit, in the birds of the air, in leaves of grass, in yeast and pearls and salt. Jesus saw the Father and was devoted to him because he was in touch with life. Jesus touched life as he touched the blind and the lepers, the children and the dead. He touched John, the faithful disciple, and Judas, the betrayer. He let life touch him. Mary Magdalen touched him, Thomas, the doubter, and the soldier who broke his heart. Jesus was devoted to the Father because he saw life rather than things, mystery rather than possessions, something to serve rather than something to own.

Jesus made an act of faith for all of us when his poetic heart, filled with devotion, prayed in contemplative wonder and loved in suffering and triumph. Jesus will never be found by those who reduce faith to words or doctrines or who limit religious behavior to moral actions or spiritual exercises. One sees rightly with the heart, and the human heart seeks to die for that which it loves. It seeks to give without reserve until it is exhausted and becomes, thereby, a total gift to another. Christianity is an affair of the heart, an experience that preserves our childhood, a process of being young all the time with wishes, and hopes and dreams, a celebration of innocence and beauty with tears and laughter, the means of grace which inspires men to make poetry of life, devotion of human relationships, contemplation from silence and patience.

Jesus experienced the same human experience we undergo. He became Christ not because he did different things but because he saw so much in all the things we ourselves know and live. Jesus ran as a child along the dusty roads of Nazareth into the mountains where he prayed as a man. He sailed the Sea of Galilee and, in Jerusalem, spoke of his body and blood, of his Easter glory and of the Spirit who was yet to come.

Jesus was born a child so that he might know at first-hand that which his disciples must never lose. He was a child so that he might learn to wonder. Jesus was God's poet; God's way of expressing devotion to us. Jesus was the contemplative prayer of a Father who was lost in wonder at his Son and filled with love for his Son's brothers and sisters.

5

In the Mountains at Night: Prayer

Prayer is an act of faith which allows hope no limit. Prayer is not a question of words; it has little to do with frequency or formulas. Prayer is an abiding influence, not because one perseveres tenaciously with a specific spiritual exercise; it is an abiding influence because something permanent has happened to the human heart. Prayer is our way of admitting we have used life to hurt; it is an effort to consecrate ourselves to healing and rejoicing. At times, we need formal prayer so that we might verbalize what has happened to us and so that we might focus explicitly on God.

Prayer is a simultaneous recognition of limitation and the limitless. Before one can pray well, he must come to terms with the limitation of his resources and the limited objectives his life can achieve. Many today are paralyzed in terms of the good they can do because they do not see how this good will renew the world or reform the Church. One loses hope the more wishful he becomes about the immediate cosmic consequences of his life.

Hope requires of us the humility of knowing that the dreams we have for mankind and for ourselves depend upon the resources of life rather than upon the achievements of one lifetime. Prayer is the expression of a heart which has devoted Its resources to the Father in commitment to the human family; it is offered in the unshakable hope that life will accomplish its meaning and achieve its destiny. Prayer comes from the awareness that one need not be present to behold the effects of his life on others and yet it derives from the conviction that one's life has already made a difference. Prayer requires a theology of the limited objective accepted in limitless hope.

Prayer does not occur in the heart of a man who thinks God will do it all or who supposes he himself can do nothing. Prayer is a willingness to admit we can do something even if not everything and that, although nothing is done without God, God does nothing without us. So often in our theology of prayer we have articulated half-truths. We have emphasized the vertical dimension of prayer and neglected its horizontal character. We have used prayer to make too much of God, too little of ourselves. We have turned away from life in the foolish notion that one could, thereby, discover the God of life. We have judged the value of prayer by the amount of time given to it rather than by its intensity.

Prayer, we have said, must be, on occasion, formal in its expression. By this, we do not mean we must follow a certain form or that prayer must be artificial to be real. We mean that prayer is not the same as human relationships, although it is influenced by them. Prayer is not the same as the work we perform, although the work we do is often the measure of what prayer has meant for us. Prayer is formal in its expression when we find explicit words and explicit thoughts to celebrate God in an explicit manner. A man never loves a woman unless he finds explicit thoughts with which to express this love in explicit words with her explicitly in mind. Prayer is an effort to keep faith from slipping into vague feeling, an attempt to come to terms with more than our everydays and to address ourselves to life as a totality.

Many of the norms we have used before to measure the adequacy of prayer must be put into proper perspective. Mystical experience is as accidental to prayer as miracles are accidental to life. Mystical experience and miracles are lesser gifts than "ordinary" life. Life needs neither of these to survive or develop. The Gospel loses little of its meaning if little is made of the miracles of Jesus. The central fact of the Gospel is the fact that Jesus is a man, the Word is made flesh, the Son of God has an "ordinary" human life to live. The Incarnation needs neither miracles nor mystical experiences to stand as the pivotal moment of history. Mystical experiences and miracles are accidentals. This is not to say that they are unimportant but merely to say that they are not essential.

Prayer can be linked with the whole range of life-experiences which constitute an "ordinary" life. One may pray when a child is born to him, on the day when a love passes from his life. He may pray when he brings opposing parties to understanding, when he pleads for peace, makes love, opens his eyes, ends his day. One may pray not only on his knees or in familiar words but as he lights a birthday candle, opens a gift, hears a footstep on the stair, a ring of the phone, or as he offers wine, breaks bread, gathers flowers.

Prayer is intimately joined to the attitudes and values of a man's life. A man who has the wrong outlook never prays; he merely says prayers. Nothing in him prays. One does not pray when he says the right words, but when he lives for the right reasons. One need not be successful in what he hopes to achieve in life in order to pray well but he must be seeking to achieve something worthwhile, something which is near poetry, devotion and contemplative wonder. When we divorce prayer from life-style, we wind up with the anomaly of the person who "prays" much but who offers no consolation, no hope, no friendship, no joy, no meaning to any other. We have considered already some of the attitudes one must be committed to if prayer is to emerge from his heart. If we wish to know where we are in life, we might ask ourselves a number of questions derived from this consideration.

What are we waiting for in life? What in life are we willing to be patient about until it comes to pass? Have we ever waited for anything which has taken time to become what it has to be for us? Is there yet something in life worth a lifetime of waiting, something or someone we will wait for all the days we have left to us?

We have spoken of the need for vivid memory. What do we remember about life with love? What do we recall when we become contemplative, thoughtful, nostalgic, joyful? What are the memories which help tie our lives together, memories which make us realize that life does not begin to be significant in the future? We have lived through, have we not, childhood and youth, sunshine and evening, every season of the year, love and tenderness, faith and tears. We have already laughed. We know what that means. We have expressed ourselves, been given a name which others have remembered, beheld the heavens, and walked the earth.

We have spoken about the standards we utilize to measure life. Jesus, we declared, drew these standards from the strength of life itself. What makes us happy, intensely happy? Is it love? Is it life? Is it friendship? Is it the human heart or the accuracy of a computer? Are we encouraged be-

cause we believe in someone or because we have won a point? Do we rejoice because we have denied ourselves for the sake of another or because we have outwitted with our cleverness a fellow human being?

What do we wish for? What are the hopes which stir us, the dreams which inspire us? Who is at home with us? With whom are we at home? What home-coming do we yearn toward? Do we hope that we might be for each man what he needs us to be for him? Are we able to keep our coming death from taking away the joy of life? Do we hope that we might someday give forgiveness without being asked? Where is home? Who is my family? How many brothers have I been given? Do we hope that one day we might go forth into a world where every man has hope in his heart?

We cannot pray well until we hope and dream and even, on occasion, wish for the right things. How can a man turn to God in prayer when his life has made a waste of the life of others? What does a man have to offer God when his heart has held only one life? How can a man look to God when he has never turned from himself?

To become sensitive to prayer we must become attuned to the mystery by which God reveals himself. The Father has made revelation from creation. He reveals by showing us dawn and dusk, by filling the sky with golden sunlight and the earth with colored leaves, noon and snow, rain and flowers. One begins his communion with God when he becomes alive to seas and sounds, human warmth and human love.

The revelation of God does not begin with his Word or his Son. It reaches its clarity in Christ. It begins, however, with creation. Those who are blind to the gift of creation and the gift of life do not perceive the fulfillment of revelation in light.

Prayer, then, is built upon a spirituality of attitudes and values rather than upon functions or exercises. It is the expression of the poetic value of the human heart, of its devotional energy, and its contemplative potential. Prayer finds expression as spontaneously as joy or pain; it is the irrepressible word we utter everytime we come home.

The man who prays raises the question of what the limits of hope may be. Prayer is his way of declaring that the boundaries of life and the limits of hope cannot be drawn with the crayons of time and space. The man who prays pushes hope into areas where men who never dream never venture. And so it is not difficult for him to believe. He believes his prayer reaches God and that it influences reality although never in a strict cause-effect relationship. Prayer is successful not in terms of what it logically produces or pragmatically achieves but in terms of what it forces reality to experience.

Prayer gives strength and insight. It supports those who go beyond human hopes and human reasons. Unless one prays, he is likely to dream not at all or to dream only of what shall actually come to pass or to dream only of what is humanly possible. Hence God, who is not humanly possible, becomes unreal; providence is dismissed as magic, heaven as medieval, hope as wishful thinking, life after death as the invention of the emotionally weak. Prayer helps us wait for the right things and never to forget them when they are given.

If this be true, prayer reaches our lives as we begin to do things we could not have done unless we had prayed. We begin to believe, we seek forgiveness, we love those who would otherwise have been unlovable to us, we attend to the important things in life. Prayer is not a pious addition to things we would have done anyway. It is a force allowing things to happen which could not have occurred without it. Jesus could not have gone to the cross unless he had first prayed in Gethsemane.

Prayer is a unifying factor in our lives, binding together poetry, devotion, and contemplation, transforming wishes into hopes, hopes into dreams, dreams into reality. Prayer inspires us to serve the mystery of man and the mystery of God. It makes us reasonable but not with human reason, volitional but also grace-conscious. Prayer is a venture beyond boundaries, an exploration in search of beauty, an expedition in eagerness for something or someone worthy of more devotion, more love, more sacrifice, more hope.

How does one learn to pray? He learns with his flesh and blood, with his eyes and his hands, with his heart and the breath of his body. He learns to pray reaching for love in the night, by not wasting the sunlight, by never allowing Spring to pass unnoticed. We learn to pray when we read the Gospel and begin to see in life what Jesus saw there.

Jesus is the first syllable man prays. Jesus is the Spirit's way of uttering "Abba", "Father" in us. This Jesus who teaches us to pray is not only the involved man of his time but the poet, alone, contemplative, in the mountains at night. This Jesus dreams of what shall never be and, in prayer, finds courage to accept what must be. Jesus, alone, in the garden, at night, finds strength to ascend Calvary and to breathe hope into the darkness of men's hatred and into the painful inevitability of his own death.

6

Jerusalem: With Words of Forceful Wisdom

On the day when we first utter a word, something significant has occurred.

We struggle an entire lifetime to say what is inside us. We begin simply, on the first day when we speak.

As life goes its way, we use everything at our disposal to make ourselves clear. Gestures and words, touches and tears, sexual love and poetry, labor and flowers, music and candles and embraces tell others that we are here. In these efforts, we say what we are like, ask for understanding, remind others that we love and hurt, that we need and dream, that we are bewildered and joyful, decisive and immediately uncertain, desperate and suddenly independent.

No struggle is equal to the struggle to let ourselves be known and to learn in the process who we are. We speak of our memories and our scattered wishes, our broken hearts and unfulfilled marriages, our disappointed children and our better years. We recall our youth, wonder out loud about age, bring forth photographs, show a wedding ring, tell where we wish to be buried. Sooner or later, we say it all. We describe a painful operation, a close call, a phobia, a foolish fear, a deceased friend, a lost lover, an unforgettable book. We speak with stardust in our eyes, with the beginnings of tears, and the faint suggestion of a smile. We speak with our hands and with our body, with an excited voice or a sorrowful face. We try at times and the words choke us, begin again and look helplessly for others to understand that sometimes words are impossible and that we need so much compassion that we cannot devise a word or a sign to call for it.

We struggle an entire lifetime and death always comes too soon. We never seem to have said it all. We do not wish to die because we suppose we might say it better if we had more time, another chance, one last effort. We wish to live so that we might sit someone still and tell it all or love someone more so that he will remember how much he meant to us. Sometimes the act of dying becomes a way of saying one more word. We give our life to save another, rush into danger to defy the senseless force which destroys us. We die with words begging people to forgive us, to remember us or to forget us, pleading for someone to see what we were really all about, asking for pardon because it takes us so long to die.

The struggle to express ourselves begins in a dramatic manner when we learn to speak. Most people sense the significance of that first day when we utter a word. Parents are thrilled and friends coax the infant to speak again. As each one hears the infant use words, he knows that something worthwhile has happened.

On the day when we first utter a word, we begin a history of countless words, listening to ourselves, hoping others will hear. We begin by calling the names of those we love. We call for our mother and our father, brothers and sisters, a favorite aunt, a frequent visitor. We say our own name and understand how much it is ours. We learn that we can speak our own name but that we cannot call for ourselves. No one else comes when we say our name. Since we do not choose to be alone, we call other names and smile as they come to us.

On the day we first speak a word, we have learned to express ourselves in a way an animal does not. An animal speaks with physical motion and sounds. We speak a word. We do not use a physical sound to say who we are or what we want but a conventional sign. We employ a language formulated by our fellow-men to speak our identity. In this, we show our relationship with and dependence upon a community, a culture, and a moment of history.

An animal makes the same sound to declare its presence in every age and in all cultures. A man is different. He reveals the concreteness of his life and its historical dimension by his manner of speech. The first day he utters a word, he declares his inseparable unity with those who taught him to speak. An animal does not learn how to create the sounds it needs to identify itself; a man, however, must listen carefully; he must have someone teach him to talk. As he speaks words, those who hear him sense a communion, a new bond, with this hitherto wordless person who now formulates familiar words.

Indeed, the sound of a person's voice becomes dear to us. Our voices are so distinctive that no one of us speaks the same way as another. The sound of our voice becomes a blessing to those we love. In moments of crisis, the sound of a leader's voice can give us strength and fill our hearts with hope. In an hour of desperation or loneliness, the voice of the right person can transform us. Even as we die, the voice of someone who meant life for us can assure us we are not lost, we have been heard, we are safe, we shall not die altogether.

Jesus struggled a lifetime to say what was inside himself. He too learned a language. He was taught to speak, corrected in his errors, encouraged when he got it right. Slowly, painfully, the mystery of the human word took root in his life. He who would one day speak the beatitudes put his first sentences together ungrammatically. This Jesus whose human words would awesomely reveal God once stammered as did we. He blushed at his mistakes and flushed with success when he overcame them.

No less arduously, Jesus struggled his entire life to say what was inside him. A great deal was at stake in his self-expression. And self-expression is never easy, never cheap, never sudden, never effortless. The human words of Jesus became means of self-identity but also sacramental realities. Through them, grace was given, revelation clarified, redemption achieved. Not only the love of man for woman, or bread and wine but human language was transformed by Jesus into a sacramental mystery. In addition to water and oil, syllables and sentences became a means of consecration and formed a bond between the Father and us.

There is an intimate relationship between the words we speak and the fidelity to which we aspire. A man's word is sacred. It guarantees the promises he makes, the vows he confesses, the oaths he takes, the commitments he honors. We receive a man's word as the expression of his inner worth, his character, his identity. When people accept our words, we know that they have accepted us. We are deemed worthy when men trust our words even without proof and believe in our promises merely because we have made them.

We have said that something significant occurs on the day we first utter a word. We create on that day the raw material by which our fidelity will be signified and the elements which will enter into the substance of our promises and vows, our oaths and commitments. We begin in a distinctive manner the history of our self-expression, a process which demands the mystery of fidelity for its completion.

Fidelity is the consistency of a person with that which is most himself. The nature of man is other-oriented. Everything in him cries out for completion in someone else. No man is faithful to himself until he has achieved fidelity with another. The consistency of a person with himself is, therefore, inseparable from his unity with another.

Although promises and commitments are part of our lives, they are not as fundamental a reality as fidelity. The validity of every promise we make is premised on a prior commitment to our own fidelity. Our words become the means by which we help create consistency in ourselves and express fidelity to others. The words we utter are so sacred that we offer them to God and invite man to trust them, even to build a life of meaning on them. Every man who loves a woman gives his word as his sign of love and declares that word, if he be a man of faith, in the presence of God, inviting his fellow-men to witness how much he loves this woman and how deeply she trusts his word.

Modern man is intrigued with the mystery of fidelity. Conscience is one aspect of this larger question of fidelity, an aspect we considered, in part, in *Belief in Human Life*.

Sometimes a person has achieved so sharp and incisive an insight into his identity that he can say at one moment of his life what he shall work toward for the remainder of his life. This sometimes occurs; when it does, it is a grace, provided that the person in question is working toward something consistent with his potential to give.

It may happen, however, that a man premises the meaning of his life on something not adequate to his potential, something which does not fulfill his fidelity but disrupts it. One is unfaithful not when he takes another path but if this new path estranges him from his own worth and diminishes his capacity for self-sacrifice.

This matter of fidelity is bound up with conscience, as we have said. It is an area of life where we are liable to self-deception, where selfishness can wear the mask of nobility of purpose, where rules are difficult to apply, norms not easy to set, advice almost impossible to give.

There is a deeper fidelity than the fidelity of our first commitments. It is the fidelity and consistency of ourselves with that in us which allows more self-fulfillment, more self-donation. One's first commitments often allow fidelity to develop. When they do, they must be maintained at all costs. To fail to do this is to become self-serving with life. Some who maintain their first commitments are faithful unto death in the manner of Jesus; others who maintain them may do so from fear or cowardice, from convenience or complacency. A person is faithful to himself, to God, and to others when he is in harmony with that which is best in himself. Faithfulness to one's total self and total sacrifice is the measure and meaning of fidelity.

Fidelity is an effort at speaking who we are in a permanent manner. It is formed in a dialogue between the words we speak in commitment and the reality within us which aspires to the fulfillment of our potential and the sacrifice of ourselves to others.

The fidelity of Jesus was expressed in consistency with himself and in faithfulness to the Father. All the promises and commitments of the life of Jesus were words by which he expressed total fulfillment and total donation. For this reason, the fidelity of Jesus is the sign of his innocence.

There was a day when we once learned to speak a real but uncertain first word. It said little of us. It had some significance, nonetheless, because we expressed ourselves in a uniquely human manner. As life progressed, we gave more solemn words, words of love in marriage, of vowed commitment in religious life. The mystery of fidelity demands a total self-expression in total self-sacrifice. No one of us does this perfectly and yet all of us must strive to honor this responsibility. It is not our first solemn words but the exhaustion of our hearts in love which makes us faithful.

7

A Temple Built by Human Hands: The Price of Peace is Suffering

The words of a child do not transform the lives of men; they are heard but we do not attend to them. A man comes of age when he realizes that people listen to his words and can be profoundly affected by them. The difference between the words of a child and the words of a mature man is the mystery of fidelity.

A child speaks, not always aware of how much is at issue in his words. He is too young to know that one pays a price for his words. He is not yet sensitive to the sacrifice demanded of the man who makes promises, the fidelity expected of the person who seeks to live with hope and devotion.

A child has little awareness of the fact that the words which bind him to others may also cut him off from his loved ones, his friends, from those without whom life is barely manageable. A child senses that his words make him part of the lives of other men, that they help make him one with the community of those who speak the same language, that words enable him to call upon those who teach him not only to speak but also to love.

A child does not yet realize that the same community which supports him today may crucify him tomorrow. A child knows that some may hurt him but he does not understand why they choose to do this. He is not yet old enough to suspect that some may one day seek his life not because of something he has done but because of something he once said. A child is too young to know that one pays a price for his words.

Fidelity is the measure of how much power our words shall have. Fidelity is the visible sign or sacrament of the fusion of poetry and prayer in the heart of a man. Fidelity is the reality created by a man who has come home to himself with devotion to others. When such a man speaks, one is aware, intuitively and surely, that he hears a faithful man, a just man, a prophet. One feels in the very words the presence and strength of a man who is consistent with himself and trustworthy with others. Such a man speaks and we know we are dealing with someone who has suffered and endured, someone who has taken the shock of life without stumbling in compromise and weakness. He has been faithful and his words convey his fidelity. He has been no stranger to pain in his heart. He speaks in the hope that his fellow-men may be healed and that, perhaps, his

fidelity may save them.

The just man has been many things in his life as he sought to express himself and give himself to others. He has been a poet and a clown, a prophet and a victim, a boy and a man, a harbor of safety, someone whose flesh and blood have given hope, someone who has prayed alone in the night and paused during the day when gratitude made him motionless with wonder. He is someone whose touch has healed and whose life has been ready for death many times if that too shall be asked of him.

Fidelity is the source of the transformative energy of our words. Christians believe that the steadfastness of our lives derives from God's gift of grace. Self-sacrificial fidelity is the fruit of grace; it is a fidelity unshaken and consistent despite fear and self-doubt. The sign of the faithfulness to which Christians aspire is the faithfulness of the crucified just man. In fidelity unto death, a Christian demonstrates that he is a disciple of this good man, Jesus, and that love will be proven once more mightier than death. A Christian sees his fidelity as one with the faithfulness of the forsaken man on the cross. From this, he gains strength to continue.

We do not rely on the fidelity of another unless we perceive, wordlessly, the fact that all which is to occur in this man's life has not yet come to pass. A faithful person is someone whose life has been consistent with himself until now but also someone who shall remain consistent through all the pain and doubt, the flattery and joy, temptation and resistance he shall yet encounter. Fidelity is, therefore, not only a demonstration of where a man has been; it is already a prophecy of where he shall always be.

Fidelity is linked to an uncertain future, uncertain in its specific events but not uncertain in terms of the fidelity of this man who shall not falter but prevail. Waiting and patience enter into the process of faithfulness. The just man has more than memories, more than harmony with himself in the present. He has patience for the future not far away and for the future which shall require a long time for its arrival. He has patience before this future which shall test him but not break him. He knows he shall be faithful to that which is deepest in himself, faithful to the way he shall be needed by others. His certitude derives from the grace which he expects and from the patient God in whom he believes.

A man who is faithful sees beforehand not the course of his life but the fidelity of his perseverance. He is optimistic about this even in his forsake-ness. He shall find the strength he needs until the last moment. And when he has no more moments to live, he shall pass into the keeping of someone who shall be as faithful with him as he was with others.

How can he know this? He is a poet who has seen the inside of life in contemplative devotion. He cannot explan all he has seen and yet he knows he has not been deceived. He is a poet whose poetry has become the prayer of his life. He has seen something and he shall never be the same again. He has seen that the inside of life is gift and that no faithful man shall be disappointed.

To speak with forceful wisdom is to experience conflict. To pray alone in the mountains at night is to behold more than the world can bear. The world cannot yet contain too much joy, too much goodness, too much of God. The world has not yet grown up enough to know the source of its life and to recognize who it is who saves it. The man, therefore, who comes to the world with too much innocence is a marked man. The man who has seen God too clearly is destined to die at the hands of his fellow-men. The man who hopes to redeem will one day shed his blood for that which

he seeks to accomplish.

Jesus was crucified because he saw too much. He was put to death because he lived too intensely. His vision of life blinded men to his goodness. In their blindness, they believed they saw an enemy. They did not know what they did as they crucified their hope. When light is very intense it can be experienced by us as darkness. When light is extreme we are as blind as we are in the darkness.

> He brought light to men. This light shines on in the darkness and the darkness cannot put it out. This was true light, the light that comes into the world to shine on every man. God made the world in this light but the world did not recognize him.

Men sometimes need a measure of darkness to behold the light. But there was no darkness in him. We are not yet ready for a dawn without darkness. There is tragedy but truth in realizing that we must sometimes behold the death of a man before we learn to treasure his life. So much of our knowledge comes too late. For some of us, it is only when a man can speak to us no more that we become conscious of his words. We understand what a man wanted to say when we are painfully distraught at the thought that we shall hear him no more, never again shall we hear this familiar voice. It is often in the loneliness of our desperate situation that we first become aware of how a faithful man sought to keep the loneliness away.

We make our friends suffer; sooner or later we put all our lovers to death. This is not because man is all evil but because he is not yet as innocent as he must be. We hurt others more often in our blindness than in our maliciousness. The tragedy of human life does not derive from the fact that we are corrupt but from the fact that we

often fail to see. So often we strike down those who come to us with visions and dreams. So often we become threatened by an excess of life, by the sheer power another has to love, by the grace of another life which confronts us with our own inadequacy.

The Gospel brings not only peace but a sword. A Christian, if he be truly a Christian, is not only a dancer and a poet, not only someone who is a clown and someone who celebrates life. He is someone who knows that he shall one day be a victim, that life shall be taken violently from him, that he will be stripped and beaten, misjudged and forgotten. A Christian, however, remembers Jesus and recalls that it is the Father who finally receives his life and that he brings each man home with mercy as well as judgment. One day, we shall be well judged.

Every affirmation of value we make in life is built on a measure of self-denial. A Christian is willing to suffer but not because he prefers it. He hates suffering. A Christian suffers because he knows that suffering need not be a sign of denial and that it is always the price of affirmation.

A man comes of age when he suffers precisely because he has seen the right things. He suffers not because he is physically assaulted or emotionally tormented. He suffers not because others seek to injure him. He suffers because of his beliefs.

A man of fidelity suffers for his choices. He suffers because of his freedom. He suffers because he loves. He suffers because he has seen and made a decision. He suffers because he is devoted, because he has made promises, because he must give in order to live. He suffers not because of what he has done. He suffers, in the manner of Jesus, because of who he is.

To preserve a child's vision all life long is to invite resistance. A child's vision is the beginning of peace but it brings suffering with it. This is not because there can be no peace without suffering but because the world resists visions as much as it desires them. Men are tempted to draw limits around life which are too restrictive for life's full expression.

A child sees no limits. He wonders why anything is impossible. A child believes in infinity more easily than he does in barriers. A man whose vision is composed of poetry and prayer, devotion and hope sees beyond the limits men set around life in selfishness, in fear, in cowardice. A just man suffers to make life grow more, gaining peace from the consistency of his vision, giving redemptive freedom by making life true to itself, but rushing toward death in his defiance of the demonic forces which tempt men to less.

A Christian does not accept the fact that love needs sexual expression in order to be love, that friendship must be utilitarian, that faith is measured by reason, or that hope is the equal of human potential. He does not accept the notion that man's whole meaning can be perceived in his lifetime or that death is the end of each man's future. He has little time for death and no faith in it.

The man of faith is always the man of tomorrow. He suffers today but he knows he shall be healed tomorrow. He dies at the hands of the blind but he knows that tomorrow their blindness shall be taken from them and that they too shall live.

A man of faith is a man of peace, waiting for peace, working for peace, dying for peace. He does not waste his life on conventional certitudes or human logic, on wordly prudence and self-serving caution. He does not squander his life in the fear of death or in the terror of pain. He is faithful to himself, to life, in the deepest recesses of his being, faithful with the energy of his heart and with the vigor of his inner justice.

A man of faith has judged for himself that everything may be taken from him if he seeks to be forever faithful. No matter. He enlightens the darkness even though he feels in it the chill of his own death. He yearns for tomorrow so strongly that he feels all the restrictions of today. He affirms freedom, staunch freedom, always freedom, refusing to allow his unfettered spirit to be imprisoned in a temple of flesh built only by human hands.

8

He Who Must Die: What Does One See from a Cross?

Father, that it should have come to this! What went wrong along the way? Where did I fail? These people are not that evil. I must have failed them in some way. Was I too innocent, too harsh, too concerned with avoiding the cross, too anxious for it? Father, how could anything which began so well end so badly? Father, I feel so empty. Where dId they all go? All of a sudden, there is nothing, no one. Should I have ended up with only these few, the few relatives who would gather for any man about to die? I had a mission. Was it your intention that it should have been for so few? Did I do what you really wanted me to do?

Father, have I been faithful to you, to them? What does it mean to be your faithful son? When all is said and done, did Satan reach me, touch me, influence me in some subtle, almost unconscious, barely perceptible manner? Which kingdom have I served the better? Who has been my Master, my Father, my God?

Father, so many thoughts torment me. They find their way through this awful pain. If only the agony would stop the thinking!

What does it mean to be innocent? There were times when I was angry, men I whipped, religious men I called hypocrites. Was I innocent in all of that? I wanted to be innocent. I resisted the demons. I did, did I not?

Nothing in me burned so fiercely as my love for you, my devotion to you, my need to know you were not far away. Did I expect too much of others? Maybe, they were not meant to be as consumed with zeal for your kingdom as I was. Did I demand too much? Was I too good, too right, too perfect? Would they have loved me more if I had loved them less?

What does it mean to be innocent? Not to compromise. How much I feared compromise. Never to exploit. How can I be sure? Not to choose myself over the need others have of me. But to choose anything involves the risk of choosing to be selfish. Father, you placed so much responsibility in my hands, so much authority. Was I worthy? Your son. I wanted to do it right because I am your son, their brother. I had to say so much, so quickly. And they listened so closely. Did I say it right? Did I always remember you? I wanted to give so much because I am your son. Maybe I said too much, too quickly. There were times when I could have been silent. Father, did I spoil it by speaking too much? Why am I here? Perhaps, I am on this forsaken hill because I was more attentive to my preaching than to their needs and to your will. I must have done it wrong at least once in a while. Did I do it wrong, all wrong, right from the start?

Father, have I been innocent? Will there be more faith in this world because I was here? Did I allow others the time they needed to hope? Was I attentive to the different ways men plead for love and express it? Did I force love for you to go only one way? Father, have I been innocent? I tried so hard to be. I wanted so much to be, so much.

A handful hoped in me. A handful, but good people. Father, don't let them forget me. Don't let them forget the good I did. When they say it went wrong, let someone tell them of the good I did, let someone be there when they say it went wrong. Allow them to remember me as innocent. Let my life make their lives innocent. Father, have I been innocent? If only you would answer me! Father, if I have failed, let this terrible pain serve as proof that I tried, that I never meant for it to go wrong, that I want to die right, that I need you to understand, even to forgive me where I need forgiveness, that I . . .

So many of those I met in the few years worried about being innocent. I know now what they feared. Father, the human heart is eager for innocence. Because of me, have mercy on them. Make them innocent. Make me innocent. Have mercy on me if I withheld mercy—ever. Have mercy on those who have hung me in this darkness. No, it isn't dark. The sun is still there. If I can love them, even those who nailed me to this tree, perhaps all men will become lovable to you, to me, to themselves.

Father, the time was so short. What did I do with it? I said I could forgive sins. Is that why I am here? You will forgive sins in the strength of my life, won't you? But it was so much to say. I said I could forgive sins. Yes, I was right to say it. Maybe I could have said it more gently, less as a challenge. Did I say it to the wrong people at the wrong time? I said I could forgive sins. It is true—

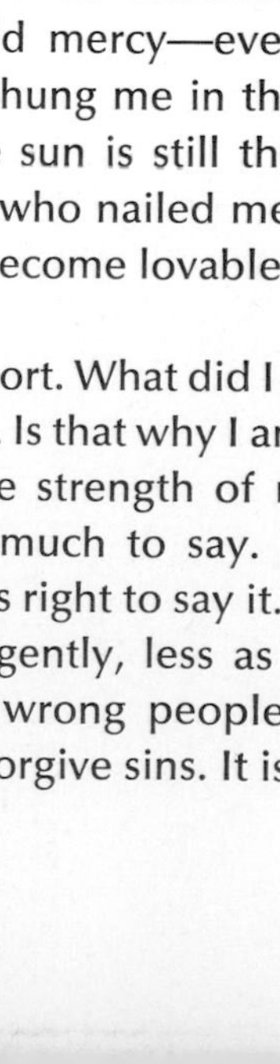

but maybe I expected too much from them in expecting them to believe it too soon.

Father, what shall become of me? Why must I die? What will you do with me after my death? What will you make of my life?

Father, so often what I had to say, what I had to be, depended upon my human choices, my sense of judgment, my limited perception. No matter who they think I was or what they think of me, they must always know that it is difficult to be a human being when so much depends on what one says, on what one does. I said I could forgive sins. Father, was I innocent? Innocence is such a big word. Forgiveness of sins is so much to say.

Father, why did I not reach them all? What did I do to fail them? Father, I worried so much about you. I had to give my life. I have no meaning unless I give, to you, for them. Did I do it right? Why did I not reach them all? Judas, what happened between Judas and me? Peter, he should have been so easy to reach. Peter, what did I do wrong? John, tell me, you knew them so well. John, am I responsible for Peter's failure, did I cut off Judas too quickly. Father, I lost so many. Even now, I lost eleven. I lost them all. What do these soldiers know of what I tried to do? Did they hear me say I could forgive sins? It's too late. I cannot reach them.

Father, they wanted to believe. Crowds followed. Wasn't the entry into Jerusalem proof that they wanted to believe? They waited for a Messiah. Why did they miss me? Father, they wanted to believe. Make my life a way of faith, a road of safety, a harbor, a home. Let my life be salvation for them.

Why did I not reach them all? Was I blameless in their hostility? How can I be innocent if I lost eleven?

Bethlehem, the desert, Galilee, Pilate, Magdalen, Mary. "Blessed are those who . . ." Father, the pain! Father, Father . . .

What must I do to die right? That is part of it too. I must die right! They will remember the way I died. Even this, Father, must make them think of you. "Father, forgive them, they have no idea. If they knew, they wouldn't." Father, forgive me if I need forgiveness.

It means so much to be faithful. But, Father, life didn't go the way I once thought it would. It changed so much, so quickly. It doesn't go the way you think it will. Father, have I been faithful? It was so different when I started out. A few years ago, I could never think I would be here. What happened from Nazareth to a crucified "King of the Jews"? "King of the Jews"! King. Imagine. I said I could forgive sins. Couldn't I have lived a little longer? Another year?

Father, I felt so close to you a few hours ago. Now, you are far away. Father, don't become a stranger to me. I lost them all but not you. If you go away, I have no one. Nothing. You're my first love, my last hope. Father, don't become a stranger to me, your son.

A few hours ago, we were so close. Bread, wine, "Remember me." John, faithful John. Peter, anxious Peter. They wanted me to stay. Vine, branches, so close. Father, make it hurt less! Make me miss them less. Make them miss me less. Father, don't let them hurt. Let me hurt—only a little less, just a little less. Father, I'd feel better if only I could be sure you loved me not only for who I am but for what I've done. Did I do it right? I said I could forgive sins. Was I innocent? Peter, you should not have gone. Peter, why did Peter leave me? How did I fail him? Why did no one stay? How could so many go? Why couldn't I reach them all? Peter . . .

A few hours ago, I was so sure. My body, this body, my body, blood, my blood, this wine. And now . . . Father, why is it so dark? Why am I so cold? Father, I'm so cold. I'm your son. I'm so cold. And the desert used to be so hot. The desert. The sands were hot. You came to me in the desert, in the sun, in the heat. Come to me now in the darkness, in the cold, in these terrible nails. Father, let me hurt—only less.

It was cold in the mountains. Father, I'm so cold. Don't let my heart be cold. Let me love them. My death will let them know I cared, how much I tried. Don't let this death be a waste. Don't let this agony fail to count. Father, I can bear the pain. I cannot bear the thought that it might be a waste, that they will not understand.

Father, your Spirit. Your Spirit must help them see the meaning of my death. I said I could forgive sins and now I'm so cold. I came to fulfill the law and the prophets. Why, then, did they turn away? When I asked if they would leave me, why did they not stay?

Father, let me feel as close, as sure as I did a few hours ago. Father, redeem me, rescue me, save me.

Father, my life. What was it all about? Did they see? Did they see anything at all? I wanted to reach them all. I wanted . . . What was it all about? Did I reach Magdalen? Will they all forget me? If I could come back, would any one remember? What was it all about? Not about death. I'm so cold. It was all about innocence, forgiveness, love. Yes, love. I said so much about love. Help me not to stop love. All the way up to the last minute, the last breath, the last effort. Help me to love all the way. Don't let my heart stop when I'm not loving. Let me love all—no exceptions. How could I forgive them all if I do not love them all?

Father, I'm so cold. Home. I'm coming home. So cold. So strange. Will home be warm? Father, don't be strange to me. Look at me, love me. Father, will you wait for me? Wait for me to die right. Father, will you understand? Father, I believe. Believe me, I believe. I believe and I hope. Father, it's so cold. Was I innocent? How can I be cold in this burning sun? I said I could forgive sins and now all I know is that I'm cold and frightened—cold and scared. Father! Where's Peter? Judas, Judas . . . I trust . . . Father, let it hurt much if it has to—only less. Father, so strange to be happy. I trust. No, it has not been a waste. Father, I'm happy and cold. Innocent. Father, it has been right, hasn't it? Innocent and cold. Father, I'm ready. Father, no more. Take me home.

9

The Lilies of the Field: And Death Shall Have No Dominion

Dawn redeems the world from darkness. It relieves the night of its harshness, leaving undisturbed those sources of light which make nighttime beautiful. One can count the stars and see the moon in the pale light of dawn. Dawn is no stranger to night; it is, however, night's redeemer.

Dawn is a sign of life. Dawn awakens the lilies of the field which flower the earth with life and, with its color, makes them less pale. Dawn is no stranger to the lilies of the field; it is the beginning of their hope for life.

Easter is symbolized by dawn and lilies. Easter is given sacramental expression in the light of dawn and in the life of lilies. Calvary is remembered in broken bread and poured-out wine. The terror of Calvary cedes to the silence and soft hope of Easter. Easter is a time for bright candles rather than burning sun. At Easter, it is dawn rather than high-noon. Easter is a time for fresh water rather than blood, a time for flowers rather than nails, for peace in place of pain, for open fields rather than for the hill of the skull. Easter heals Calvary and reveals what happens when hope is steadfast unto death.

All the world seeks freedom. Redemption is another name for freedom. But how is freedom given?

The world is not free because a man dies. The end of the life of Jesus cannot be the beginning of freedom. No freedom issues from the brokenness of the body of Jesus, no joy from his excruciating pain, no consolation from his agony in blood and cries. Freedom must not come from the fact that Jesus dies but from the fact that his death achieves something more significant than the end of his life.

Human life does not increase when men celebrate the dying of Jesus as the central event of history. Men must never celebrate death; they celebrate only life or love.

Human freedom comes from man's discovery of values which give freedom. For this reason, revelation and redemption are closely allied. We are redeemed when freedom-giving values are revealed to us. Redemption means that we have been set free from the choice of the wrong vision. Jesus gives freedom not by a static cancellation of sin but by a dynamic revelation of realities which resist evil. Redemption is the revelation to us of those values without which life will be enslaved, misdirected, distorted.

To be patient is to possess one's freedom and one's self in the whirl of circumstances which might otherwise undermine us. To be humble is to keep one's integrity and freedom while others compromise their worth to win the acclaim and the vain attention without which they cannot live. To love one's enemies is to be free of their enmity and their hatred. To be a peace-maker is to be free of hostility and vengeance. To struggle for human justice is to be free of prejudice and provincialism. To be merciful is to be free of anger or condescension. To be pure of heart is to be free to see more than an empty tomb; a pure heart is the prism through which we behold the beauty of dawn as it affects the lilies of the field.

Freedom does not come from the unrestricted use of our wills nor from the opportunity for unlimited options. It comes from an affirmation of the right values and from the incarnation of values worthy of sacrificial love.

If Jesus redeemed us by the embodiment of values equal to sacrificial love, then this is how we must redeem one another. We become sacraments of freedom to our brethren when we witness to values which men need for their freedom. This is why witness is essential. To witness is to redeem.

Jesus redeemed us not only on the cross when he revealed love without restraint. He redeemed us when he made it clear that there was a worth in celebrating the lilies of the field. The lilies were beautiful because they were seen by a man, whom we remember as our redeemer, and loved by a man, in whom we confronted the Son of God. On Easter morning, the man who beheld the lilies of

the field lived in a way where death could have no dominion over him. Jesus, poet and prophet, beheld the lilies of the field in all their beauty and was astonished by them.

Man is not bereft because there is no beauty in life but because he so seldom attends to it. We become so preoccupied with ourselves and so anxious about the success or failure of the accidental circumstances of life that we lose sight of the total reality in which we are situated.

To notice the lilies of the field is to relate to more than one's own concerns and goals. It is to be mindful that beauty is not of our making. Beauty is made as we give and receive simultaneously. It is created by the union of sacrifice and gift. It occurs when we give ourselves to something whose significance in itself, even apart from us, is striking. Beauty is conceived when the heart of man is thrilled by something to which he belongs but for which he is not totally responsible.

On Easter morning, at dawn, Jesus lived again. His victory was more than a victory over sin. It was not a victory in which he outlasted hostile forces. It was a victory in which he brought forth something significant from the darkness of his death into the dawn of his new life. It was a victory in which beauty was preserved intact, a victory in which innocence survived the stress and turmoil of a lifetime, a victory in which the lilies of the field live on forever in the Christ who cannot die.

Modern man needs a sacramental universe more than he needs a world of miracles. He desires signs which mediate the meaning of life to him. He does not require for his life extraordinary interventions, exotic demonstrations of power, stupendous occurrences. His peace does not depend upon another miracle but upon a sacramental view of life. He will be content if he can be assured there is a point to life, a beauty to everyday, a purpose to the efforts which tire his heart, scar his body, distress his spirit.

Modern man needs a poet, someone to make sacraments for him from the substance of the earth so that he can feel life again, touch it, sense its goodness, perceive its intrinsic and undying value. Modern man needs to know what dawn means before he can understand baptism. He must see the stars again before he believes in the holiness of marriage. Someone must remind him of the lilies of the field before he can celebrate the Eucharist.

Easter must be made a sacramental event rather than a miracle if modern man is to believe in it. The proclamation of a miracle excuses us from having anything further to do with it. A miracle is God's doing. A sacrament, however, makes a demand upon us for its existence. God performs miracles but men celebrate sacraments. God may work a miracle even without faith and he may work it, apart from men, in the physical universe. Man, however, is essential to the presence of a sacrament.

If Easter is to be a sacramental event, we must symbolize it for our fellow-men not only in the grace of God but with our flesh and blood. Easter is sacramental everytime one of us makes his life a source of light for his fellow-men. Easter is sacramental when our words heal, when our hearts understand, when lesser values die in us for the sake of greater realities.

Easter is not real because a preacher proclaims its presence but because men are consoled and redeemed by the life of another. Easter is real when we become sacraments of its presence. Jesus lives again, he easters in us, when men come home to themselves in our presence and when men dislike our absence because they find hope when we are nearby.

We are sacramental with Easter when men know us to be faithful. We are sacramental with Easter when our fellow-men see us suffer not for selfish advantage but for their redemption. Easter is never more sacramental than when one man gives his life on behalf of another.

Christians seek to make Easter sacramental in their lives by their memory of Jesus. If Jesus is remembered, he has not died altogether. If the memory of Jesus inspires us to sacrificial love, Jesus is grace. Jesus is an Easter-maker. He lives in us with his deathless body and his sacrificial blood and he renders us courageous for freedom by the Spirit he gives. Jesus is an Easter-redeemer whose memory is a vision for the future, whose revelation is a freedom-giving event.

Jesus is best remembered when we recall him in the midst of those who believe in him. The memory of Jesus is a community experience. We learn to speak, as we have said, because we are related to the community of our fellow-men. We learn to pray when we are related to a community of those who believe.

Jesus teaches us to pray, at dawn, near the tomb, as Easter takes root in us, enlightening the darkness of our hearts and persuading our dead spirits into life. We pray when new life touches us. We pray when we look for God in the mountains, for the Father's love in a dark garden, for life although Lazarus is buried, for nourishment although there are only a few loaves, for fish in an empty lake, for flowers in a sterile field, for Jesus in the breaking of the bread. We pray not from a sense of obligation or expecting a miracle but from a sense of life within us. We pray because we believe Jesus never dies and because Easter is born again every Spring with the lilies of the field.

Jesus is the Springtime and September of every life. He is God's Easter grace, strong enough to endure death, weak enough to need us. Jesus is God's sacrament, sensitive enough to proclaim the lilies of the field in all their glory, faithful enough to give his body and shed his blood. Jesus is God's hope for those who look for him at dawn and discover him at dusk when the hour is late and they ask him to remain. Jesus is the stranger at our side looking at us for a sign of Easter.

We who accept the Gospel must accept it all the way. We must accept its sword and its peace, its Friday bleakness and its Easter freshness. We must know that Easter is as demanding upon us as Calvary and that Easter cannot be proclaimed until we are made an Easter people.

The glory of Easter morning lives on not only in the splendor of the lilies but, more effectively, in the sublimity of bread and wine, of memory and hope which we call Eucharist. Easter is available in its demand and its peace when we remember with light and water, with grace and quiet hope, with evening vigil and early morning hours the Christ who comes to life again in our as-

sembly. Easter is a Eucharistic sacrament when we promise fidelity anew to the life of Jesus and to his commandment that we love one another with freedom, that we forgive one another with mercy, that we offer peace to one another with our lives.

Easter is the name we give to the dawn dominion of Jesus and to the hope of his kingdom which resists death. Easter is the name of fidelity when Christ enters the process. Easter is the celebration of a memory which prevails even in our forgetfulness of it.

10

A Crimson-Cresseted Morning: Waiting

It begins with waiting and it ends with waiting.

Many times we wonder why life has to take so much time, why it must move forward step by step, moment by moment. If we try to rush it, it goes wrong. Life has its own time to keep, its own unhurried pace to set. And so we learn to wait.

We wait for everything that is really worth having. We wait to be born. We wait for love to touch us. We wait for life to grow. Till the very end, we wait. We even wait for God. As we are about to die, we continue to wait, supposing that if the right person enters the room we may hear that a way out has been found and that, therefore, we shall not die. And so we wait.

Modern man is filled with expectations. No era has expected so much as has ours. We are often convinced that somewhere, somehow there is an answer to everything. We believe that man deserves a savior in every situation. We feel that man need not be a sinner, that a cure for that too will be found. We are open to the conviction that youth ought to last, that the human heart can be purified through some secular achievement, that loneliness can be banished, happiness assured. All this can be accomplished, we surmise, with good will, energy, ingenuity, and with the right generation in command.

Expectation can be the beginning of faith. A man who waits is someone who knows he was made for more. A man who waits for everything understands that he was made for everything. It is not wrong that man expects so much. It is wrong when we have a time-table for the fulfillment of our most profound expectations. It is wrong when we look for one lifetime to settle the human heart, quiet its every fear, meet its expectations, and end its waiting. There is beauty and meaning in our waiting if we can sort out in our own minds what we are waiting for, whom we await, why we wait.

Jesus, who was no stranger to hope, was also no stranger to waiting. He had to wait even though everything in him may have questioned why this had to be and what purpose this waiting served.

We are made to wait because hope and faith are at issue in our waiting. If we wait for nothing, faith is impossible and hope is unnecessary.

We wait so that we may know that all does not originate with ourselves, not even the meaning

of our lives. We wait so that other persons might participate in the process of our lives. We wait because the resources we require to survive and grow have not been given into our individual keeping.

And so we wait. We wait for home-coming, partial strangers to all the moments of life, never entirely settled into the homes we build, straining toward the future in the hope of a family we have not yet found in a home beyond the horizon of our present vision.

In the life of Jesus, God reveals to us the need to wait. Along the dusty roads of Nazareth, Jesus waits with a child's vision and a child's prayer, with a child's eagerness for the future. A carpenter and a prophet, he waits in the mountains at night, with a young man's sense of dedication and mission, with a dreamer's impatience to know what life expects of him and whether he can accomplish it.

Jesus waits as a preacher, beginning his ministry and wondering how he shall be heard, if he is saying it rightly, whether any will listen. Jesus waits for the human heart to catch up with him. He waits for Peter to weep and return, for Thomas to join the disciples and set aside his doubt, for the Emmaus pilgrims to recognize him.

Jesus also waits for his own heart to learn the story of man's sad and glorious journey through time. As he waits, his heart receives human experience with grace and love, with cries of pain and shouts of joy.

The human heart is not built in a day. It takes a lifetime to make a human heart. It takes it all: birth and learning how to talk, making wishes, living with hope, dreaming dreams. The human heart is nourished with yearning for tomorrow, with poetry and devotion, with contemplation and the incessant thought of home. The human heart prays; it strives to find a faithful lover; it does not love until it dies in fidelity for the mystery of another life.

The human heart suffers or else it does not grow; it exhausts itself or else it is empty; it waits and hopes, at dawn and dusk, in darkness and daylight.

The human heart is not built in a day nor can it be built alone. The human heart loses its way unless it receives the promises of others and gives its trust in return. It needs bread to break, wine to consume, memories to cherish, lilies to hold in the hand. The human heart waits or else it does not live and yet it dies waiting. It breathes the air of hope and is suffocated in despair.

Jesus waits. His waiting is active and significant but it demands discipline as waiting always does. He waits to see how his contemporaries will react to him. He waits to know whether he shall indeed become the Messiah for his people. As he waits, he is charged and convicted by some of those whom he loved, in whom he hoped. On the cross, he waits. Apparently alone, he searches the heavens for a Father and for the meaning of this waste of his life. Unable to find an answer, he waits, near desperation, no longer in control of his own destiny, helpless to help himself. Jesus dies waiting. Death comes before the Father. Jesus waits and he dies.

What do we remember about this Jesus, this unsuccessful Messiah, this crucified poet, this silent prophet? What can one recall of a vanquished life? Everything he hoped to accomplish met defeat. The most bitter moment of all is the aftermath of a shattered dream.

He had a dream for a kingdom of love, this carpenter with nails in his hands. He assembled a community of hope around him, this king of the Jews with the tears still wet on his face. He came with a message, with beatitudes by which to live and bread and wine with which to celebrate. He gave promises, of God's Spirit, of life forever, this man who loved life and who looked vainly for those he loved just seconds before he uttered a cry of near despair and certain death.

What is there to remember? Must we remember that all good men come to this, that innocence invites its own destruction, that every ardent hope is crucified, that the Father who gives life deserts even his beloved Son when he pleads for life? What is there to remember? Shall we remember with bitterness the fact that there is no place for a kingdom of the human heart, for a kingdom for the hopeful and the lovers of life, for a kingdom with God as its center, for a kingdom of memories

and dreams, for a kingdom for all the tomorrows of the world, for a kingdom built at dawn and visible to the eyes of faith? There shall never be another Jesus. If Jesus could not establish such a kingdom, no such kingdom shall ever be built.

For those who can wait no more, there are no further kingdoms. For those who have tired of patience, all expectations have regressed to memories. Memories without dreams give no life. Memory is vitalized by expectations.

If Jesus failed, how shall we succeed? If Jesus died beyond recall because a handful of men could not bear him, what shall become of us who are less than Jesus? In the defeat of Jesus, every poet reads the death of his own hopes. In the broken, beaten body of Jesus, every innocent man reads in advance the destiny of all Innocence.

Some will wait no more. And so they live not by choice but by supposed necessity with the conviction that every good thing in life will have a beginning but no worthwhile end. They number the death of their hopes and watch their dreams dissolve into despair. Those who will wait no more see all the beauty of the world flower for a desperate moment and fade into insignificance.

If we choose instead to wait, we must realize that at times the waiting may seem endless. Sometimes the waiting will occur in the darkness. But every man waited once in the darkness for his birth to be accomplished. Life manages in the darkness to take strong root and to await dawn. Even in the darkness, there is a worth to waiting.

We wait because we have seen the inside of life and we know that life never waits for nothing. We wait with the sign of the cross upon us and with an Easter hope in our hearts. We wait because we are strong in the memory of all that life has been. We wait for the lilies to come again and for Jesus to return. We wait with bread and wine, with the words of Jesus in mind and with his Spirit to give us patience.

Some say we are foolish to wait. No life comes forth from a tomb; no one survives crucifixion. Death gives life no second chance.

A Christian, however, chooses to wait. He waits because he knows that life grows in the daylight and in the darkness. He realizes he was once born from the silence and the darkness and he is willing to wait through even the silence and darkness of death to be born once more. A Christian waits because he knows that if he despairs of waiting and loses hope in the darkness he shall have missed all the lessons life teaches us about darkness and its relationship to life and to birth.

A Christian waits because he has seen the lilies, the wheat fields, and the stars. A Christian waits because he knows that darkness is not for death but merely one way to wait for morning. A Christian waits because he knows that even the darkness is a creature of God and that no darkness can withstand dawn.

The author

Photograph: The Record, Hackensack, N. J.

Father Padovano was born on September 18, 1934 in Harrison, New Jersey, attended Seton Hall University and the North American College in Rome. He was ordained with the Class of 1960 at the North American College and received two graduate degrees in the same year from Roman Universities (S.T.D. and Ph.L.).

Presently, Father Padovano is Professor of Systematic Theology at Immaculate Conception Seminary at Darlington, New Jersey, and has taught courses at Villanova, St. Mary's College at Notre Dame and the University of St. Thomas in Houston, Texas. In addition to his teaching, he is a weekend Assistant at a Church in the Archdiocese of Newark and has traveled throughout the country during the past three years giving talks and lectures in almost every State and at almost every major theological and philosophical meeting.

He is a member of the National U.S. Dialogue Group for Lutheran-Roman Catholic Theological Conversations and was one of the twelve members of the national committee responsible for the document on Due Process accepted by the Canon Law Society of America and the National Conference of Catholic Bishops. He is also a consultor to the National Catholic Office for Radio and Television.

Previously published books: The Estranged God (Sheed and Ward, 1966); Who is Christ? (Ave Maria Press, 1967); Belief In Human Life (Pastoral Educational Services/Paulist Press, 1969); American Culture and the Quest for Christ (Sheed & Ward, 1970). Articles published in Magazines: Guide, Catholic World, Ave Maria, Christian Century, National Catholic Reporter, Sign and Preaching. Theological Papers published: Anglican Concept of Episcopacy (1964); Mary, Mother of the Church (1966); American Unbelief and the Death of God (1966, v.21 Proceedings of Catholic Theological Society of America); Original Sin and Christian Anthropology (1967 v.22 Proceedings of Catholic Theological Society of America).